ॐ

SANSKRIT DEVANAGARI FONT

Open Type Design, Indic Shaping & Spell Check

Ashwini Kumar Aggarwal

जय गुरुदेव

© 2021, Author

ISBN13: 978-81-950754-8-5 Paperback Edition
ISBN13: 978-81-950754-7-8 Hardbound Edition
ISBN13: 978-81-950754-4-7 Digital Edition

This work is licensed under a Creative Commons Attribution 4.0 International License. Please visit
https://creativecommons.org/licenses/by/4.0/

Title: **Sanskrit Devanagari Font**
SubTitle: **Open Type Design, Indic Shaping & Spell Check**
Author: **Ashwini Kumar Aggarwal**

Printed and Published by
Devotees of Sri Sri Ravi Shankar Ashram
34 Sunny Enclave, Devigarh Road,
Patiala 147001, Punjab, India

https://advaita56.weebly.com/
The Art of Living Centre

https://www.artofliving.org/

21st January 2021, Dipanshu at TIET 34th Convocation, Guruji's 1st Satsang after Bangalore Ashram reopens on 2nd Jan 2021
Pausha Shukla Paksha Ashtami, Ashwini Nakshatra, Uttarayana
Vikram Samvat 2077 Pramadi, Saka Era 1942 Sharvari

1st Edition January 2021

जय गुरुदेव

Dedication

Sri Sri Ravi Shankar

who infuses Faith in all of Creation

Blessing

All that you can do is to raise the level of Sattva. And then when Sattva's level is high, we have to wait one moment, any moment knowledge can dawn there.

All that you can do to have sunlight in this room, is to open the curtains and keep the windows open. And when dawn comes, it just dawns. You have the sunlight inside.

Sri Sri Ravi Shankar
A discourse on Yogasara Upanishad

Contents

BLESSING 4
PREFACE 9
PRAYER 10
TECHNICAL TERMS 11
PRIVATE USE BLOCK 12

    Devanāgari Half Forms 13
    Devanāgari Half Forms with Halant 15
    Devanāgari Half Forms for Repha 16
    Devanāgari Half Forms needing Implementation 17
    Desirable Conjuncts for clarity and conciseness 18

ANCIENT DEVANĀGARI GLYPHS 19
ALTERNATE GLYPHS 19
REPHA रकार 20

    Repha with vowelsign उकार / ऊकार 20
    Repha with vowelsign ऋकार / लृकार 21
    Repha when 2nd letter in Conjunct 21

UNICODE CHARACTER SETS FOR VEDIC SANSKRIT FONT 25

    Devanagari – 0900 to 097F 26
    Vedic Extensions – 1CD0 to 1CFF 26
    Devanagari Extended – A8E0 to A8FF 26

ADDITIONAL CHARACTER SETS NEEDED 27

    Basic Latin U+20 to 7E (95/95 characters) 27
    Latin-1 Supplement U+A0 to BE, F7 (approx 32 characters) 27
    Latin Extended-B U+0192 27
    Spacing Modifier Letters U+02BC (approx 4 characters) 27
    Greek and Coptic $03BC (1 character) 27

Tibetan U+0FD5, 0FD6 (2 characters) 27

General Punctuation U+2009 to 203A. (approx 22 characters) 27

Currency Symbols U+20A8, 20AC, 20B9 (approx 3 characters) 28

Letterlike Symbols U+2122 28

Mathematical Operators U+2212, 2219 28

Geometric Shapes U+25CC 28

Private Use Area U+E000 onwards 28

TRANSLITERATION GLYPHS FOR DEVANĀGARI TO LATIN 29

Proposal for Final a = अ 29

Extra Characters Needed 31

IAST 33

ISO 15919 34

IAST and ISO 15919 Differences in encoding characters 35

Unicode Blocks used by IAST and ISO 15919 35

Latin-1 Supplement – A0 to FF 35

Latin Extended A – 0100 to 017F 35

Latin Extended Additional – 1E00 to 1EFF 35

Combining Diacritical Marks – 0300 to 036F 36

Redundant Glyphs earlier used for Transliteration 37

DEVANĀGARI GLYPHS IN A SANSKRIT FONT 38

Repha Conjunct Glyphs 38

Use of Zero width Joiner Glyphs 38

Use of Dotted Circle Glyph 39

Devanāgari Atomic Consonants 39

Devanāgari Vowels 39

Devanāgari Matras (dependent vowel glyphs) 39

Devanāgari Halant for Half Form of Consonant 40

Devanāgari Anusvara and Visarga (dependent glyphs) 40

Devanāgarī Digits 40
Devanāgarī Punctuation marks 40
Devanagari Special Symbols 41
Devanagari other Language specific Letters 41

KEYBOARD MAP FOR VEDIC SANSKRIT TYPING 43

OPEN TYPE DESIGN CONSIDERATIONS 50

INDIC SCRIPT DEVANAGARI 50
INDIC SHAPING FEATURES 51
AboveBaseMarkPositioning (abvm) 55
AboveBaseSubstitutions (abvs) 64
Akhands (akhn) 66
BelowBaseForms (blwf) 67
BelowBaseMarkPositioning (blwm) 68
BelowBaseSubstitutions (blws) 72
ConjunctForms (cjct) 75
HalantForms (haln) 77
HalfForms (half) 78
MarkPositioning (mark) 79
MarkToMarkPositioning (mkmk) 79
NuktaForms (nukt) 79
PostBaseSubstitutions (psts) 80
PreBaseSubstitutions (pres) 82
RakarForms (rkrf) 83
RephForms (rphf) 84
VattuVariants (vatu) 84

DEVANAGARI CHARACTER GLYPH CLASS SCHEME 87

Devanagari Block = Unicode U+0900 to 097F 89
Vedic Extensions Block = Unicode 1CD0 to 1CFF 91
Devanagari Extended Block = Unicode A8E0 to A8FF 93

FONT PROGRAMMING - CORRECT PLACEMENT OF ACCENT, MATRA, BINDU, NUKTA USING ANCHORS 95

    Sample Typing using Sanskrit 2020 font 97

POSITIONING 4 OR MORE GLYPHS 108

    Use Composite glyph rather than combining 108

CHALLENGES OF INCORRECT LIGATURES 109

    Svarita Accent Placement with Top Repha 109

    Svarita Accent with Anusvara 109

    Anudatta Accent with Visarga 109

    Anudatta Accent with Bottom Matra/Conjunct 110

    Dirgha Svarita Accent Placement with TOP Matra 110

SAMAVEDA ACCENTS 'ADD SPACE BEFORE/AFTER PARAGRAPH' 112

CHANGES NEEDED IN THE SHAPING ENGINE 113

    Gomukha Anusvara U+1CE9 113

    Heavy yya U+097A 113

    Ardhavisarga U+1CF2 113

    Numeral १ and ३ Accents 114

    Numeral २ Tones U+1CD0 114

    Accents for Candrabindu Virama U+A8F3 115

    Nasalized semivowel 115

INDIC SHAPING AND SPELL CHECK REQUIREMENTS 116

SHAPING TECHNICAL TERMS IN UNICODE 121

REFERENCES 126

EPILOGUE 130

Preface

Boys hope and achieve the impossible.

A single Soul can change the landscape and the fortunes of the entire planet.

Men may come and men may go, but the boyish Spirit remains alive and indomitable, nay incorrigible.

Prayer

शान्तिपाठः

ॐ सह नाववतु । सह नौ भुनक्तु । सह वीर्यं करवावहै ।
तेजस्वि नावधीतमस्तु मा विद्विषावहै ॥
ॐ शान्तिः शान्तिः शान्तिः ॥

oṃ saha nāvavatu I saha nau bhunaktu I saha vīryaṃ karavāvahai I tejasvi nāvadhītamastu mā vidviṣāvahai II
oṃ śānti śānti śāntiḥ II

Peace Invocation
O Pure Loving Grace!

May we be taken care of along with our family and friends.
May we enjoy socializing and eating together.
May we support each other's vision and growth.
May our intellect be open to new ideas and changing trends.
May we spend more time in praise than abuse, may we talk of each other's virtues rather than harp on vices.

Peace in our heart, in our body and in our environs.

Technical Terms

Character = a Unicode space holder. E.g. U+0905

Glyph = a Symbol or Sign or Ligature that is drawn in the Unicode Character space. E.g. अ

Ligature = a combination of Glyphs. E.g. ङ्क्

Symbol = an independent Glyph. E.g. क

Sign = a dependent Glyph, that attaches to another Glyph. E.g. ौ

Ayogavaha = an extra nasal or breath sound produced during speaking. For Devanagari texts, it is ideal to have written symbols for such sounds. E.g. ȯ

Allographs = Language specific glyph change is known as allograph.

Private Use Block

This is an important section in Unicode, whereby we can directly see and insert any glyph of the font using MS Word. So it is a must in a Vedic Sanskrit font Sanskrit 2020/Advaita Sanskrit, that has many conjuncts and alternate letters/glyphs.

Helps in Teaching Grammar.

E.g. U+1CE9+0902 Gomukha Anusvara that should combine with Bindu. ॐ ॐ ॐ ॐ ॐ ॐ ॐ ॐ ॐ ॐ

E.g. Rigveda Accented Numeral. १॑ ३॑

E.g. U+1CEA+0902+1CED Gomukha Anusvara that should combine with Bindu andTiryak. ॐ

E.g. U+A8F3+0951 Long Anusvara that should combine with Accents. ॐ॑ ॐ॒

E.g. Half Forms that otherwise cannot be typed. व् रु ज् द् ड्

E.g. Stylistic or Alternate Letters that otherwise cannot be typed. प ट ह रु रू त

E.g. Conjuncts. ज्छु स्स्य

E.g. Top Repha etc. ꣳ ꣴ ि॑ िः

Devanāgari Half Forms

Independent Half Forms क़ख़ग़च़ज़ढ़ऱङ़ण़थ़ध़ऩप़फ़म़य़ऱऴ़ल़व़श़ष़स़

Half Forms customarily with Halant ङ्‌छ्‌ट्‌ठ्‌ड्‌ढ्‌द्‌ह्‌

Vedic Sanskrit ऴ्‌ ऱ्‌

Half Conjuncts ह्‍ह्‌

Open Type Design in Font Editor uses code HalfForms (half)
- Zero Width Joiner character U+200D
- Replacing resultant glyph with suitable glyph from Private Use Area block

क + ् + $200D = क् → क़	च + ् + $200D = च् → च़	ट + ् + $200D = ट्‌
ख + ् + $200D = ख् → ख़	छ + ् + $200D = छ्‌	ठ + ् + $200D = ठ्‌
ग + ् + $200D = ग् → ग़	ज + ् + $200D = ज् → ज़	ड + ् + $200D = ड्‌
घ + ् + $200D = घ् → घ़	झ + ् + $200D = झ् → झ़	ढ + ् + $200D = ढ्‌
ङ + ् + $200D = ङ्‌	ञ + ् + $200D = ञ् → ञ़	ण + ् + $200D = ण् → ण़
त + ् + $200D = त् → त़	प + ् + $200D = प् → प़	य + ् + $200D = य् → य़
थ + ् + $200D = थ् → थ़	फ + ् + $200D = फ् → फ़	र + ् + $200D = र् → ऱ
द + ् + $200D = द्‌	ब + ् + $200D = ब् → ब़	ळ + ् + $200D = ळ् → ऴ
ध + ् + $200D = ध् → ध़	भ + ् + $200D = भ् → भ़	व + ् + $200D = व् → व़
न + ् + $200D = न् → ऩ	म + ् + $200D = म् → म़	
श + ् + $200D = श् → श़	ऴ + ् + $200D = ऴ्‌	क्ष + ् + $200D = क्ष् → क्ष़
ष + ् + $200D = ष् → ष़	य + ् + $200D = य् → य़	ज्ञ + ् + $200D = ज्ञ् → ज्ञ़
स + ् + $200D = स् → स़		
ह + ् + $200D = ह्‌		

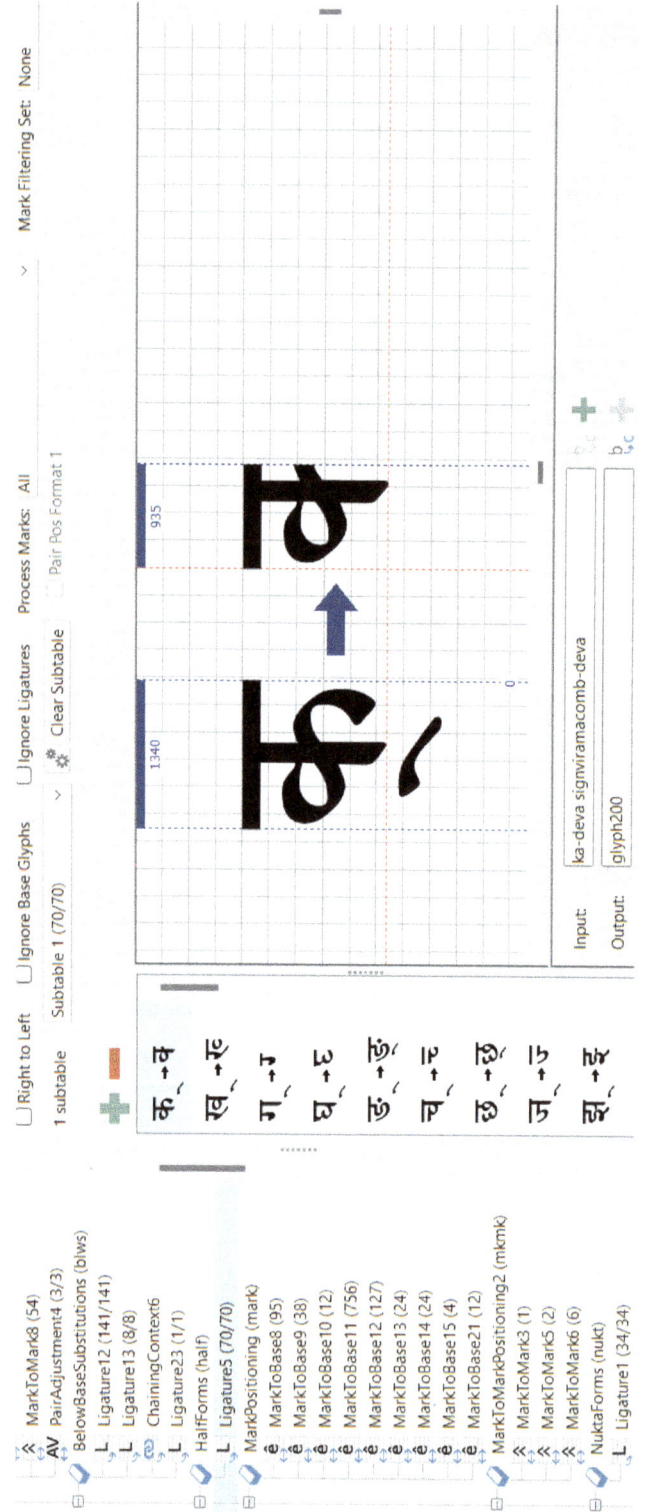

Devanāgarī Half Forms with Halant

Half Forms customarily with Halant ङ़्‌छ़्‌ट़्‌ठ़्‌ड़्‌द़्‌ह़्‌ uses code HalantForms (haln)

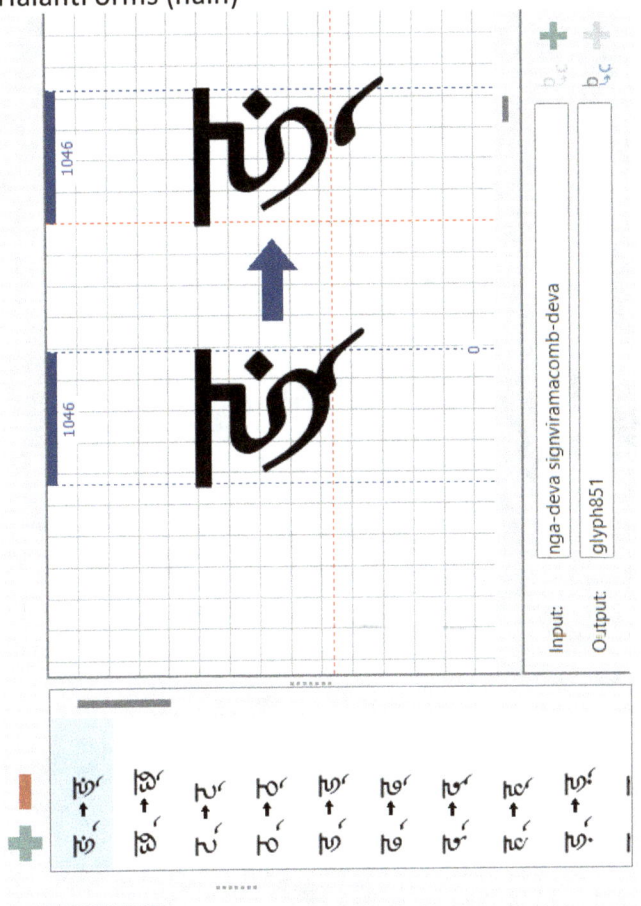

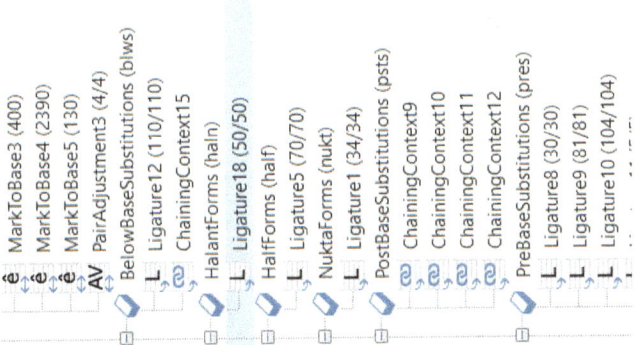

Devanāgari Half Forms for Repha

Repha has its own independent code RephForms (rphf)

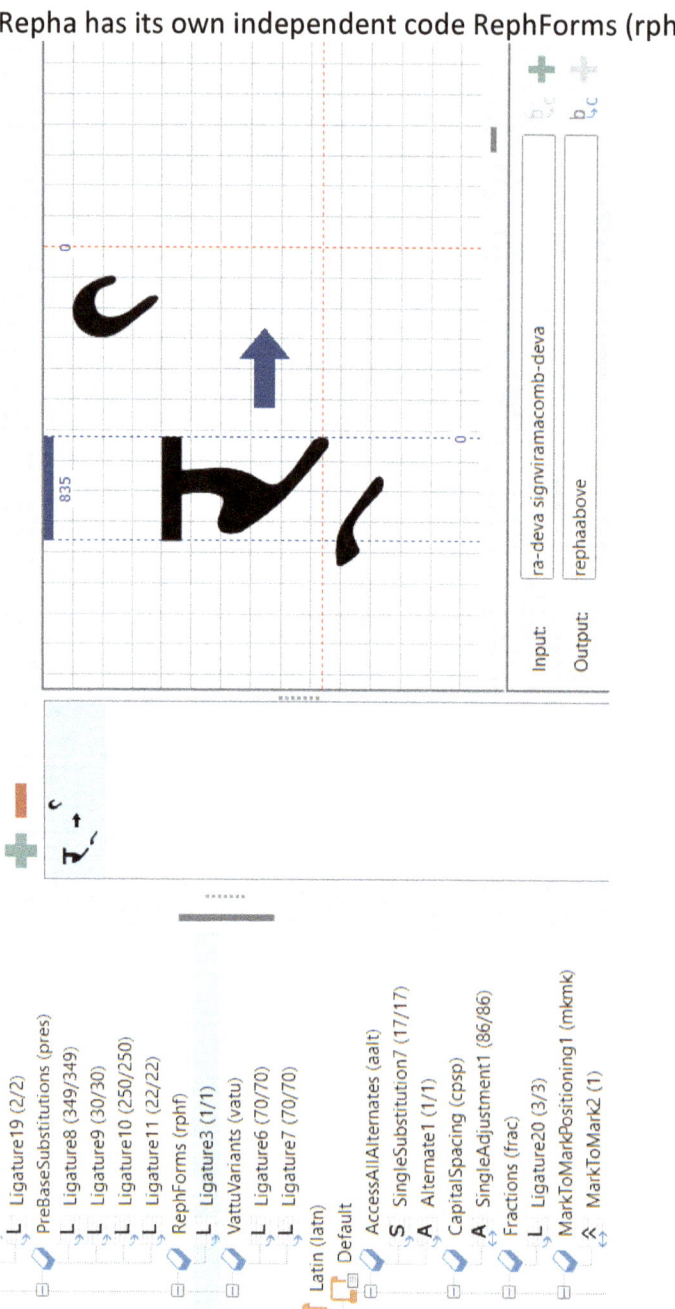

Devanāgari Half Forms needing Implementation

Note: The Vedic character U+097A Devanagari Heavy ya य़, has not so far been accounted for by the Indic Shaping Engine code Halfforms (half). Hence it does not allow the Halant ् to get attached while typing on the keyboard.

It has been implemented using BelowBaseSubstitutions (blws).

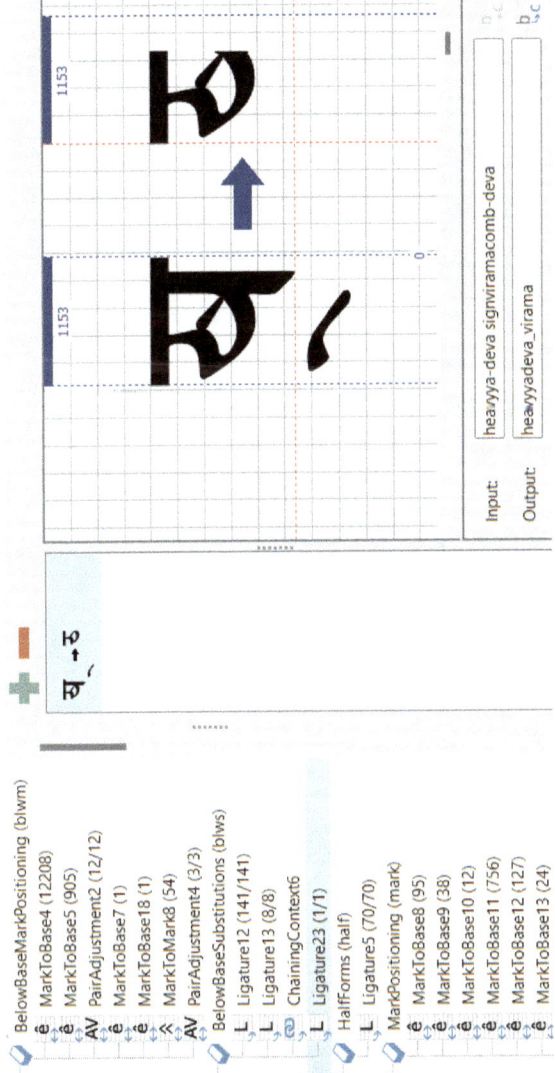

Desirable Conjuncts for clarity and conciseness

A list of desirable ligatures for beautiful Devanagari typesetting that prevents confusion and has clear readability.

स्न स्न स्न

क्त्व क्त्व

ध ध

Ancient Devanāgari Glyphs

In ancient texts some glyphs are seen which have been superseded in recent texts by newer glyphs. This is also known as Allograph.

Ancient / Recent vowels			
ꢲ / अ	ꢲा / आ	ꢲो / ओ	ꢲौ / औ
Ancient / Recent consonants			
ꠙ / झ	ꠚा / ण		
Ancient / Recent conjuncts			
ꠛ / क्ष			
Ancient / Recent half-forms			
ꠜ / इ	ꠝ / ए	द् / क्ष	
Ancient / Recent numerals			
ꠞ / ५	ꠟ / ६	६ / ९	
U+094E ◌ Vowel Sign Prishthamatra represented ए while combining			
◌ + ए → ऐ	◌ + आ → ओ	◌ + ओ → औ	
U+094E · Sign high spacing dot			

Alternate Glyphs

Sometimes we wish to use an alternate form of a letter or glyph during teaching or for clarity.

श / श	इ / इ	ॐ / ॐ	ध / ध	न / न

Repha रकार

Repha with vowelsign उकार / ऊकार

Customarily 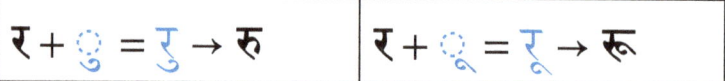 is used for repha instead of

र + ु = रु → रु	र + ू = रू → रू

The code BelowBasesubstitutions (blws) is used.

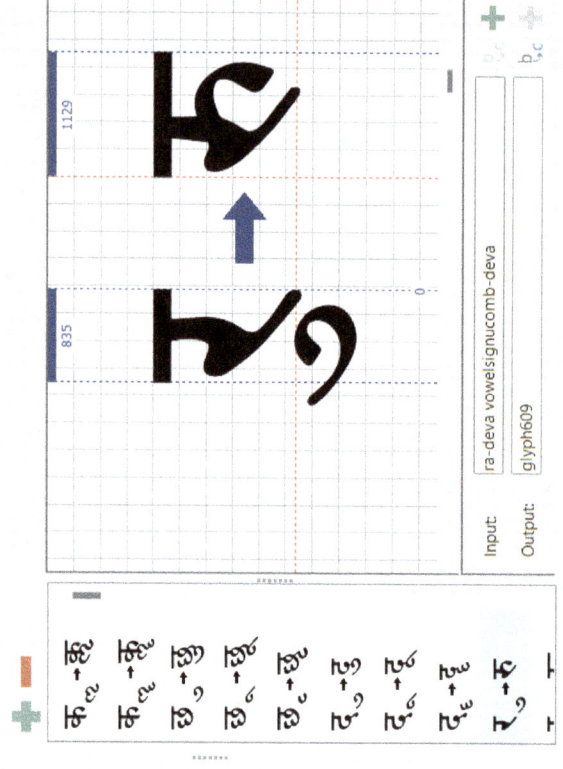

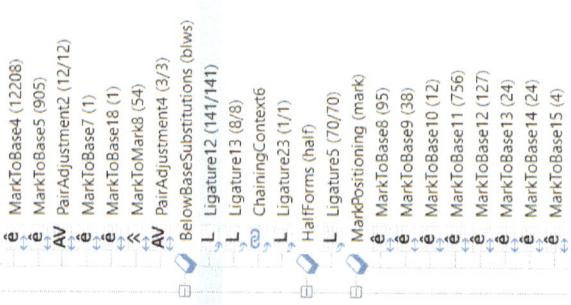

Repha with vowelsign ऋकार / लृकार

Both forms are prevalent रॄ / ऱॄ

र + ◌ृ → रृ / ऱृ	र + ◌ृ → रॄ / ऱॄ
र + ◌ॢ → रॢ / ऱॢ	र + ◌ॣ → रॣ / ऱॣ

Repha when 2nd letter in Conjunct

In such cases, there are three distinct forms of repha, ◌ॆ र

क + ◌ + र → क्र
ट + ◌ + र → ट्र
र + ◌ + र → र्र

2nd letter Repha as a short slash क ख ग घ च छ ज झ ञ प ण त थ द्र ध न प फ ब भ म य व श ष स ह I Encoded in two steps, BelowBaseForms (blwf), and then VattuVariants (vatu) in Open Type Design.

2nd letter Repha as a circumflex below ड ट ठ ड ढ ळ छ स I Encoded in single step BelowBaseForms (blwf) in Open Type Design.

2nd letter Repha as Repha र्र I Encoded in single step RephForms (rphf) in Open Type Design.

2nd Repha as a circumflex below ऱ

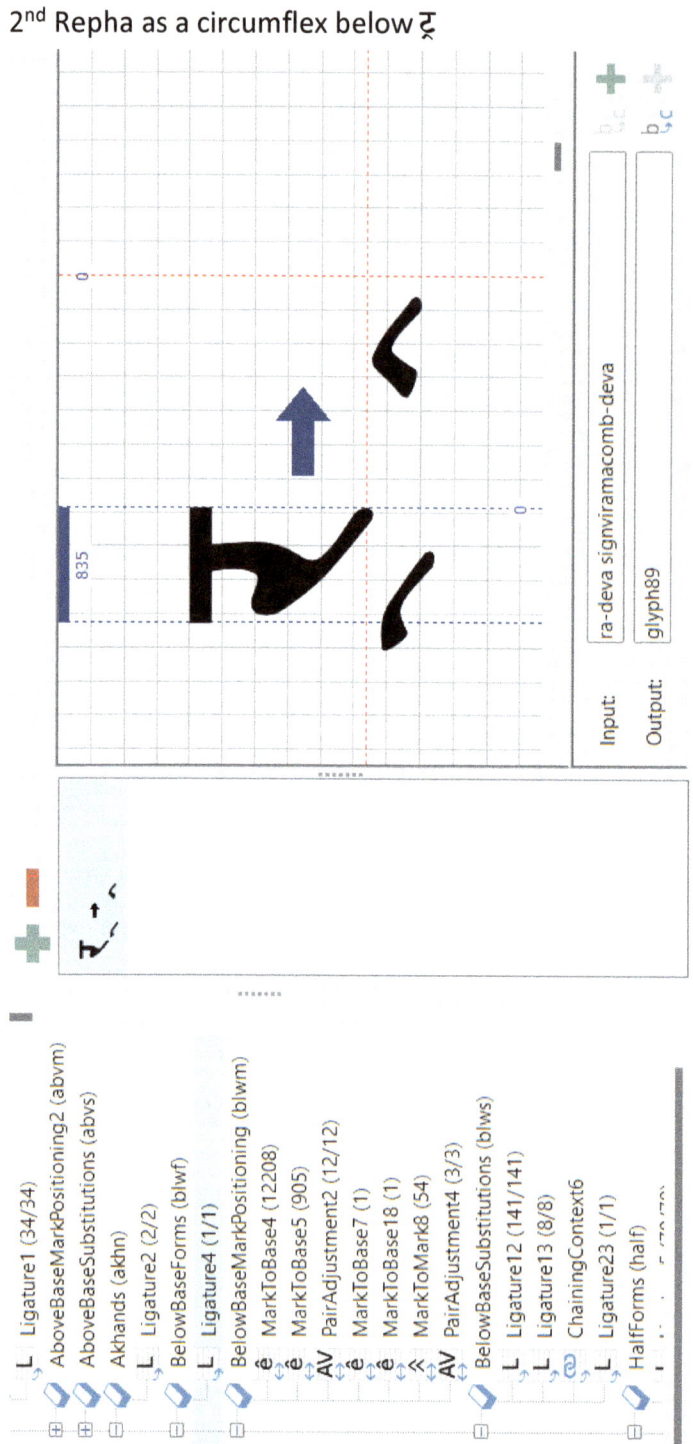

2nd Repha as a short slash क

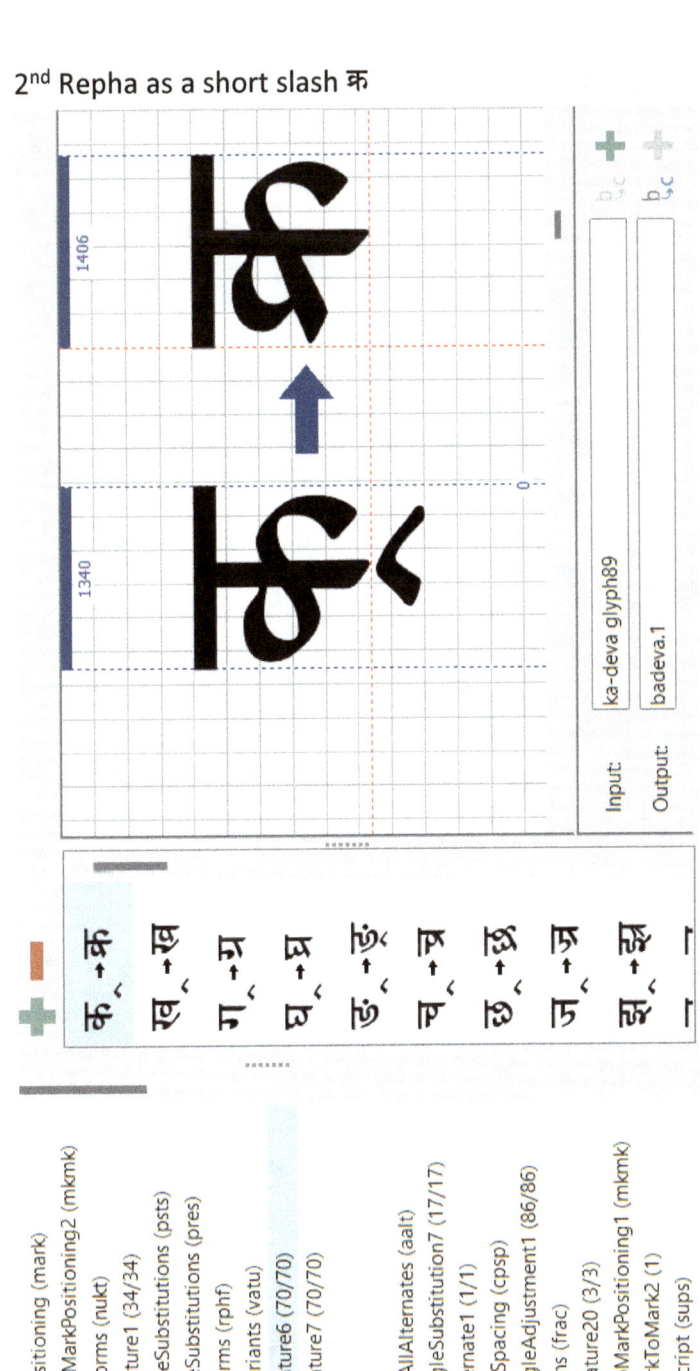

2ⁿᵈ letter Repha as Repha र्

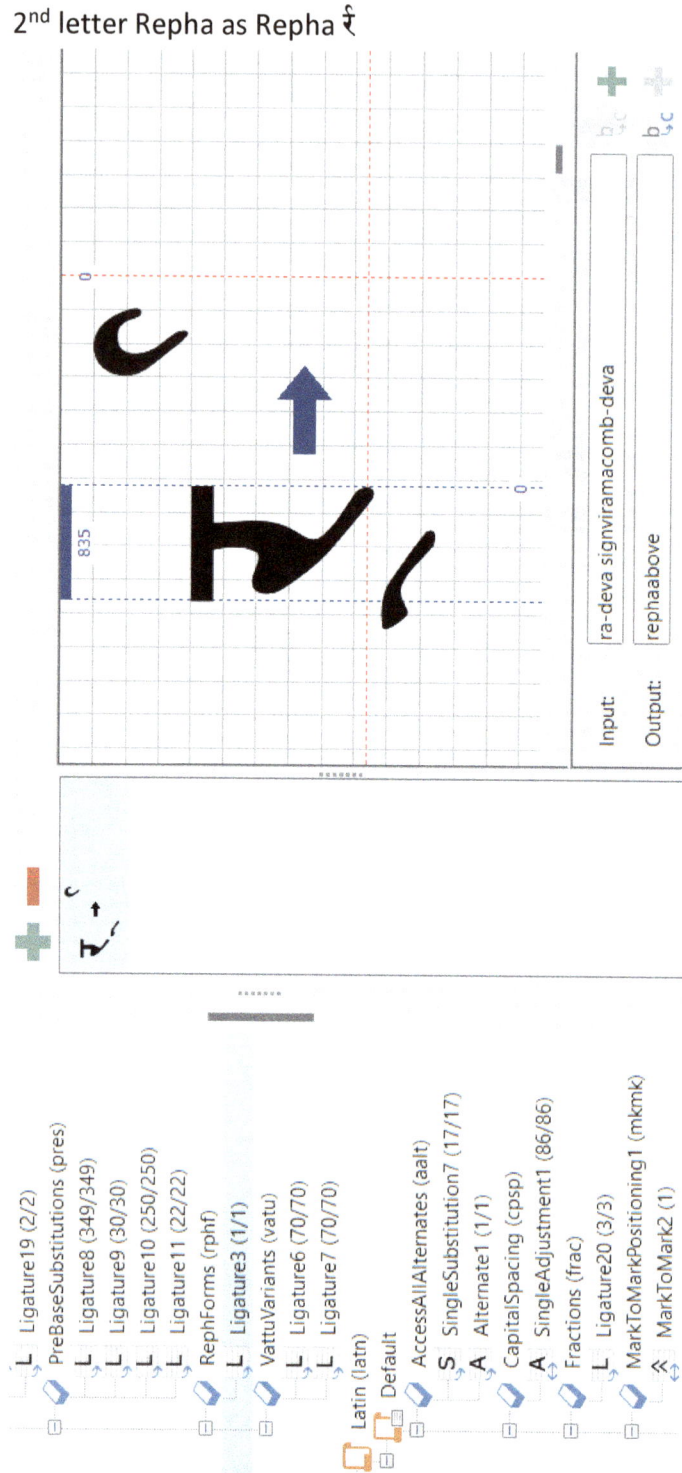

Unicode Character sets for Vedic Sanskrit Font

To design a complete font to serve the purpose of typesetting Vedic Sanskrit texts and classical Sanskrit texts, the Unicode character sets needed are:

- Devanagari U+0900 to 097F (128/128 characters). Some characters here are for languages other than Sanskrit, e.g. Marwari, Dravidian, etc.
- Vedic Extensions U+1CD0 to 1CFF (43/48 characters, last 5 unallocated). All 43 characters are needed.
- Devanagari Extended U+A8E0 to A8FF (32/32 characters). Few characters here are for other languages.

Apart from these, we shall need:
- Basic Latin U+20 to 7E (95/95 characters).
- Latin-1 Supplement U+A0 to BE, F7 (approx 32 characters).
- General Punctuation U+2009 to 203A. (approx 22 characters).
- Currency Symbols U+20A8, 20AC, 20B9 (approx 3 characters).
- Letterlike Symbols U+2122.
- Mathematical Operators U+2212, 2219.
- Geometric Shapes U+25CC.
- Private Use Area U+E000 onwards. For many glyphs, including half-forms, conjunct ligatures, ligatures to support typesetting where Open Type shaping engine is not correctly implemented in Editor or typing software, etc.

Note: For Devanagari to Latin transliteration, many encodings are prevalent, including IAST, Velthius, ISO15919, Harvard-Kyoto, etc. These have relied on Latin Extended-A U+0100 onwards, and Latin Extended Additional U+1E0C onwards. However these are rather incomplete to do Vedic Texts which have many Accents.

We propose a new Unicode block for the same, or collecting all the requisite glyphs in the Private Use Area block.

Devanagari – 0900 to 097F

Characters used in Sanskrit Language, Vedic and Classical.

Vedic Extensions – 1CD0 to 1CFF

Out of 48 characters, 43 characters 1CD0 - 1CFA have been allocated and are in use. The last 5 characters 1CFB - 1CFF are unallocated in Unicode Standard Version 15.0 dated Sept 2022.

Devanagari Extended – A8E0 to A8FF

Out of 32 characters, initial 24 are in fair use in Sanskrit literature. Of the last 8 characters A8F8 – A8FF, some are punctuations seen in ancient texts, and the last two are vowels used in Hindi/Awadhi or other languages.

A8F8	꣸	Sign Pushpika (punctuation/paragraph marker)
A8F9	꣹	Gap Filler (punctuation)
A8FA	꣺	Caret (punctuation to indicate missing letter)
A8FB	ꣻ	Headstroke (Vedic Sanskrit)
A8FC	꣼	Sacred Sign Siddham (Ancient texts)
A8FD	ꣽ	Sacred Jain OM (Jainism texts)
A8FE	ꣾ	Letter AY (languages other than Sanskrit)
A8FF	ꣿ	Vowel Sign AY (languages other than Sanskrit)

Additional Character sets needed

For making a robust and complete Devanagari font for typesetting Classical and Vedic Sanskrit, some additional Unicode character sets are needed. Most of these character sets are needed partially only, except for Basic Latin which is needed in toto for the font to function well.

Basic Latin U+20 to 7E (95/95 characters)

Latin-1 Supplement U+A0 to BE, F7 (approx 32 characters)

Latin Extended-B U+0192

U+0192 *f* small letter f with hook, used for Windows encoding.

Spacing Modifier Letters U+02BC (approx 4 characters)

U+02BC ʼ U+02C6 ˆ U+02C9 ˉ U+02DC ˜ Used for Windows encoding.

Greek and Coptic $03BC (1 character)

U+03BC µ Greek small letter Mu, used for Windows encoding.

Tibetan U+0FD5, 0FD6 (2 characters)

U+0FD5 卐, U+0FD6 卍 svasti = sacred symbols for well-being.

General Punctuation U+2009 to 203A. (approx 22 characters)

Currency Symbols U+20A8, 20AC, 20B9 (approx 3 characters)

U+20A8 ₨ Rupee Sign

U+20AC € Euro Sign

U+20B9 ₹ Indian Rupee Sign

Letterlike Symbols U+2122

U+2122 ™ Trademark

Mathematical Operators U+2212, 2219

U+2212 − minus sign

U+2219 ∙ bulleted list operator

Geometric Shapes U+25CC

U+25CC ◌ dotted circle, used by Indic Shaping software to indicate some mark glyph is missing a base glyph for attachment.

Private Use Area U+E000 onwards

For many glyphs, including half-consonants, special ligatures, conjunct ligatures, ligatures that are a part of typesetting Vedic Sanskrit and are as yet not encoded in Open Type Design Indic Shaping software, etc.

Transliteration Glyphs for Devanāgari to Latin

We use glyphs from various Unicode character sets for efficient transliteration.

One thing to note is that Transliteration is needed to enable non-native readers of Sanskrit Devanagari script to read correctly using Latin transliteration. However this transliteration must NOT jeopardize the pronunciation for native speakers of Sanskrit.

In particular, the transliteration for final 'a' of a word i.e. the final devanagari letter that does not have any vowel sign attached, must be carefully transliterated. Otherwise, the native speakers shall mispronounce it as 'aa', thus distorting the Sanskrit language entirely. In a Devanagari font, a new character that suppresses 'long a' when uttering words having 'a' at end. E.g. Lord Ram vs Rām vs Rāma. One thing is accuracy in transliteration for foreign speakers, however if it changes pronunciation for native speakers, that is a grave anomaly and must be addressed forthwith.

Proposal for Final a = अ

We propose the glyph "ᵃ = U+1D43 Modifier letter small a" that will be used in Latin transliteration for 'final a = अ in a word'.

- राम योग रामायण सूर्य मोह विवेक वैराग्य Vairāgyᵃ
- Characterᵃ, e.g. Rāmᵃ, Yogᵃ, Rāmāyaṇᵃ, Suryᵃ, Mohᵃ, Vivekᵃ

Alternative Transliteration proposals:
- This can be 'a' in extra light font, e.g. Rāma, Yoga
- This can be 'a' in 4 points lower font size, e.g. Rāma, Yoga
- This can be 'a' in gray shade font, e.g. Rāma, Yoga

Perhaps then it shall not elongate the 'a' for native speakers when reading/speaking aloud the text.

Transliteration Glyphs

We see that English has 26 letters of the alphabet, while Sanskrit has 56 letters of the alphabet. Which means we can map only 26 letters directly, and we shall need 30 extra characters for representing the remaining letters of Sanskrit. Hithero people have used Unicode supplement and extended blocks. We propose that the Private Use Area block can be efficiently used while developing a new Sanskrit Font for the same.

English Alphabet 26 letters
a b c d e f g h I j k l m n o p q r s t u v w x y z

Sanskrit Alphabet 56 letters

- 14 vowel letters
  अ आ इ ई उ ऊ ऋ ॠ ऌ ॡ ए ऐ ओ औ
- 3 ayogavaha letters
  ं ः ँ
- 33 consonant letters
  क ख ग घ ङ च छ ज झ ञ ट ठ ड ढ ण त थ द ध न प फ ब भ म य र ल व श ष स ह
- 2 Vedic Sanskrit consonant letters
  ळ य़
- 1 ardhavisarga
  ᳵ Vedic Sanskrit ayogavaha letter (ideally we must use this same glyph for transliteration from the Vedic Extensions block, instead of finding a new glyph).
- 3 long anusvara
  ँ ᳲ ᳳ Vedic Sanskrit ayogavaha letters (ideally we must use the same glyphs for transliteration from the Vedic Extensions and Devanagari Extended blocks).

Note: Sanskrit has additional symbols for accents, diacritics, etc., those have not been covered in transliteration just yet, as that is not a significant need for any non-native reader for regular texts.

Extra Characters Needed

Extra characters needed apart from Basic Latin Unicode block for Devanagari transliteration.

Note: Transliteration shall follow the English scheme of **caps and no caps**, hence two glyphs per Sanskrit letter.

Sanskrit Letter	Latin Transliteration Character		
	Transliteration with CAPS and no caps		
	IAST	Unicode	ISO 15919
आ	Ā ā	U+0100, U+0101	Ā ā
ई	Ī ī	U+012A, U+012B	Ī ī
ऊ	Ū ū	U+016A, U+016B	Ū ū
ऋ	Ṛ ṛ	U+1E5A, U+1E5B	R̥ r̥ U+0052+0325, U+0072+0325
ॠ	Ṝ ṝ	U+1E5C, U+1E5D	R̥̄ r̥̄ U+0052+0325+0304, U+0072+0325+0304
ऌ	Ḷ ḷ	U+1E36, U+1E37	L̥ l̥ U+004C+0325, U+006C+0325
ॡ	Ḹ ḹ	U+1E38, U+1E39	L̥̄ l̥̄ U+004C+0325+0304, U+006C+0325+0304
ए	E e	U+0045, U+0065	Ē ē U+112, U+113
ओ	O o	U+004F, U+006F	Ō ō U+014C, U+014D
Existing transliteration schemes have two letters for each of these, we have proposed a single new letter			
ऐ	AI ai	U+0041+0049, U+0061+0069	AI ai
औ	AU au	U+0041+0055, U+0061+0075	AU au
ऍ	Æ æ	U+00C6, U+00E6	Proposed
ऑ	Œ œ	U+0152, U+0153	Proposed
Perhaps no caps is needed here since no word begins with it – an ayogavaha letter coming at the end of a word, however CAPS is given for Uniformity during teaching			
ः	Ṃ ṃ	U+1E42, U+1E43	Ṁ ṁ U+1E40, U+1E41

◌ः	Ḥ ḥ	U+1E24, U+1E25	Ḥ ḥ
◌ँ	~	U+0303 e.g. ॐ OM̐ om̐	M̐ m̐ U+004D+0310, U+006D+0310 e.g. ॐ ŌM̐ ōm̐
ऽ	'	U+0027	'
Vedic Letters			
ऌ	Ḷ ḷ	U+1E3A, U+1E3B	Ḷ ḷ U+1E36, U+1E37
य़	NA		Y̌ y̌ U+0059+030C, U+0079+030C
◌×	NA		H̱ ẖ U+0048+0331, U+0068+0331
◌×	Propose ◌× the same glyph for transliteration		
ॐ ◌ ◌	Propose ॐ ◌ ◌ the same glyphs for transliteration		

Note:
ISO 15919 can be encoded using the Unicode Blocks
- Basic Latin and Combining Diacritical Marks

or we may use the Unicode Blocks
- Latin Extended-A and Latin Extended Additional

The encoding for Avagraha ऽ is ' U+0027 = apostrophe character. It is not the character given on standard laptop keyboards ' U+2018 = Left single quotation mark.

IAST

International Alphabet of Sanskrit Transliteration (IAST)

0101		012B		016B	1E5B	1E5D	1E37	1E39
a	ā	i	ī	u	ū	ṛ	ṝ	ḷ	ḹ
अ	आ	इ	ई	उ	ऊ	ऋ	ॠ	ऌ	ॡ

				1E43	0303	1E25	NA	1E43
e	ai	o	au	ṃ	~	ḥ	Ardha Visarga	oṃ / oṁ
ए	ऐ	ओ	औ	◌ं	◌ँ	◌ः	◌×	ॐ

Consonants shown with vowel 'a = अ' for uttering

ka	क	ca	च	ṭa	ट	ta	त	pa	प
kha	ख	cha	छ	ṭha	ठ	tha	थ	pha	फ
ga	ग	ja	ज	ḍa	ड	da	द	ba	ब
gha	घ	jha	झ	ḍha	ढ	dha	ध	bha	भ
ṅa	ङ	ña	ञ	ṇa	ण	na	न	ma	म

ya	ra	la	va	śa	ṣa	sa	ha
य	र	ल	व	श	ष	स	ह

NA = Not Available as not currently IAST encoded. We use ISO 15919

1E3B	0027	y̌	ẖ	Note: Consonant only	
ḻa	'	NA	NA	ka	क्अ = क
ళ	S	य़	◌×	k	क्

ISO 15919 uses some combining characters

ṛ = r + U0325 ring below	r̄ = r + U0325 + U0304 macron above	ḷ = l + U0325 ring below	l̄ = l + U0325 + U304 macron above

m̐ = m + U0310 ̆ candrabindu above	
y̌ = y + U030C ̌ caron above	ẖ = h + U0331 _ macron below or U+1E96

ISO 15919

International Standards Organisation for Devanagari Transliteration

	0101		012B		016B	0325	0304	0325	0304
a	ā	i	ī	u	ū	r̥	r̥̄	l̥	l̥̄
अ	आ	इ	ई	उ	ऊ	ऋ	ॠ	ऌ	ॡ

0113		014D		1E41	0310	1E25	1E96	1E41	
ē	ai	ō	au	ṁ	m̐	ḥ	ẖ	oṁ / om̐	
ए	ऐ	ओ	औ	◌ं	◌ँ	◌:	◌×	ॐ	

Consonants shown with vowel 'a = अ' for uttering

				1E45					00F1
ka	kha	ga	gha	ṅa	ca	cha	ja	jha	ña
क	ख	ग	घ	ङ	च	छ	ज	झ	ञ

1E6D		1E0D		1E47					
ṭa	ṭha	ḍa	ḍha	ṇa	ta	tha	da	dha	na
ट	ठ	ड	ढ	ण	त	थ	द	ध	न
pa	pha	ba	bha	ma					
प	फ	ब	भ	म					

					015B	1E63			
ya	ra	la	va		śa	ṣa	sa	ha	
य	र	ल	व		श	ष	स	ह	

1E37	0027	030C	1E96		Note: Consonant only				
ḷa	'	y̌	ẖ		ka	क्अ = क			
ळ	S	य	◌×		k	क्			

Note: Unicode is given for uncommon letters. (keyboard ALT+X).
ISO 15919 uses Combining Diacritical Marks, but Latin Extended may be used alternatively. E.g. ē = U+0065+0304 or ē = U+0113

IAST and ISO 15919 Differences in encoding characters

IAST

1E43	0303	1E43	1E3B			1E5B	1E5D	1E37	1E39
ṃ	~	oṃ	ḻa	NA	NA	ṛ	ṝ	ḷ	ḹ
ः	ँ	ॐ	ळ	य	◌×	ऋ	ॠ	ऌ	ॡ

ISO 15919

1E41	0310	1E41	1E37	030C	1E96	0325	0325 +0304	0325	0325 +0304
ṁ	m̐	ṁ	ḷa	y̌	ḥ	r̥	r̥̄	l̥	l̥̄
ः	ँ	ॐ	ळ	य	◌×	ऋ	ॠ	ऌ	ॡ

Sanskrit	IAST	Unicode	ISO 15919	Unicode
ए	e	U+0065	ē	U+113
ओ	o	U+006F	ō	U+014D

Unicode Blocks used by IAST and ISO 15919

Some characters from the Supplement and Extended blocks are used by the transliteration schemes. These Unicode blocks are:

Latin-1 Supplement – A0 to FF

Latin Extended A – 0100 to 017F

Latin Extended Additional – 1E00 to 1EFF

Then we have the Combining Diacritical Marks block, most of these characters cannot be typed directly from the keyboard, rather we need to use Insert-Symbol-More Symbols and choose the font and the subset, find the requisite character and insert it.

Combining Diacritical Marks – 0300 to 036F

IAST and ISO 15919 Devanagari to Latin Transliteration characters

Unicode	Symbol	Meaning	Remarks
0027	'	Apostrophe	S avagraha
Note: Keyboards have U+2018 ' Left single quotation mark			
0303	~	Combining tilde above	oṁ IAST
Note: Keyboards have U+007E ~ Tilde			
0304	ˉ	Combining macro above	ē
0307	˙	Combining dot above	anusvara
030C	ˇ	Combining caron above	y̌ ISO 15919
030D	ˊ	Combining vertical line above	Vedic svarita
030E	˝	Combining double vertical line above	Vedic dirgha svarita
U+030D and U+030E are not used in Transliteration, rather they may be used to type Vedic Sanskrit in absence of Vedic Extensions block			
0310	̐	Combining candrabindu above	candrabindu
0323	.	Combining dot below	ṃ
0325	ₒ	Combining ring below	r̥ ISO 15919
0331	ˍ	Combining macron below	ḻ IAST

Redundant Glyphs earlier used for Transliteration

U+0953 Devanagari grave accent `

U+0954 Devanagari acute accent ´

These glyphs are no longer in use since they do not have Indic shaping properties in Open Type design code. Just present to maintain continuity with earlier versions of Unicode when Sanskrit to Latin transliteration used these symbols. These are now superseded by symbols U+0300 ` Combining grave accent, U+0301 ´ Combining acute accent. However, even these symbols are not seen in transliteration.

Devanāgari Glyphs in a Sanskrit Font

Open Type design that uses Indic shaping engine rules exhibits the given features. Only the glyphs used for Sanskrit Language typesetting are listed. (The Devanagari script is used to write many languages, not all glyphs are used by Sanskrit).

Repha Conjunct Glyphs

For the Repha, conjunct glyphs vary as per previous or next letter.
- Repha as 1st letter in a conjunct, Repha half consonant र् = र्
  e.g. RephaKakara conjunct कर्खर्गर् etc.
- Repha as 2nd letter in a conjunct ्र, e.g. KakaraRepha क् + र = क्र, similarly ख्र ग्र घ्र ह्र etc.
- Repha as 2nd letter in a conjunct, e.g. ttakaraRepha ट् + र = ट्र, similarly ठ्र, ड्र, ढ्र etc.
- Language other than Sanskrit, e.g. Marathi Repha half consonant र् = र्

Use of Zero width Joiner Glyphs

General Punctuation Unicode Block characters in a Sanskrti font.
U+200C Zero width non-joiner
U+200D Zero width joiner

क् + U+200C + त = क्‌त
क् + U+200D + त = क्त

क् + U+200C + ष = क्‌ष
क् + U+200D + ष = क्ष

Use of Dotted Circle Glyph

Geometric Shapes Unicode block Dotted Circle character in a Sanskrti font. It is used by the Indic shaping engine that uses the Devanagari script. (dev/deva).

U+25CC ◌ Dotted Circle

- This is used to indicate the presence of a dependent glyph, that is missing its base glyph for getting attached. ◌ं vs कं
- It is used to type a dependent glyph ◌ा during teaching, etc.

Devanāgari Atomic Consonants

The glyphs that are directly encoded in Unicode table are referred to as atomic glyphs, as they are directly typed without any adjustment or additional glyph. Note: These consonants have the inherent अ vowel.

Classical and Vedic Sanskrit Consonants.
क ख ग घ ङ , च छ ज झ ञ , ट ठ ड ढ ण , त थ द ध न , प फ ब भ म , य र ल व , श ष स , ह

Vedic Sanskrit Consonants ळ य

(Consonants with Nukta are used in other languages, Hindi, etc. क़ ख़ ग़ ज़ ड़ ढ़ ऩ फ़ य़)

Devanāgari Vowels

Vowels used in Sanskrit are:
अ आ इ ई उ ऊ ऋ ॠ ऌ ॡ ए ऐ ओ औ ।

Devanāgari Matras (dependent vowel glyphs)

Matras are standard for most consonants.
ा ि ी ु ू ृ ॄ ॢ ॣ े ै ो ौ

For the Repha र, there is a change in attaching the vowel matras ◌ु ◌ू
◌ृ ◌ॄ ◌ॢ ◌ॣ ।

Devanāgari Halant for Half Form of Consonant

Halant ् (dependent glyph) depicts half-form of a consonant.

क्ख्ग्घ्ङ्च्छ्ज्झ्ञ्ट्ठ्ड्ढ्ण्त्थ्द्ध्न्प्फ्ब्भ्म्य्र्ल्व्श्ष्स्ह्

Devanāgari Anusvara and Visarga (dependent glyphs)

Anusvara ं and Visarga ः are ayogavaha sounds that appear during speaking.

Devanāgari Digits

0 to 9.

० १ २ ३ ४ ५ ६ ७ ८ ९

Devanāgari Punctuation marks

बुद्धियुक्तो जहातीह , उभे सुकृतदुष्कृते । तस्माद् योगाय युज्यस्व , योग: कर्मसु कौशलम् ॥
Bhagavad Gita 2.50

Danda । represents virama = stop. (for a partial verse).

Double danda ॥ represents purna virama = fullstop. (end of a complete verse).

Abbreviation sign ॰ represents an abbreviated word. अष्टाध्यायी । अष्टा॰

Additionally, in typesetting texts in the modern era, the Latin punctuation marks are freely used, e.g. , comma, . full stop, ? question mark, - hyphen, etc.

Devanagari Special Symbols

Om ॐ sacred symbol, used at the beginning of any text.

Avagraha ऽ used in Sanskrit Grammar Sandhi to indicate अ dropped.

प्रथमः अध्यायः । प्रथमोऽध्यायः ।

Rupee symbol ₹ Indian currency (Unicode Currency block). ₹२१०० = Rs 2100.

Svasti ༄ ༅ indicates well-being for the reader, is typed at the end of a text (Unicode Tibetan block). ༄ इति ༅

Devanagari other Language specific Letters

We see that a Sanskrit Devangari font needs the Devanagari Unicode block, not all its characters are used by the Sanskrit language.

Devanagari Hindi/Awadhi language specific Letters

U+0904 ऄ vowel , U+090D ऍ vowel , U+090E ऎ vowel

U+0911 ऑ vowel , U+0912 ऒ vowel

U+093C ़ nukta sign

U+0945 candra ॅ (for omkara) ऍ ऎ ऑ ऒ

Devanagari Hindi/Dravidian language specific Letters

U+0929 ऩ nukta consonant, U+0931 ऱ nukta consonant

Devanagari Marathi language specific Letters

U+0933 ळ Also seen in Vedic Sanskrit.

U+0934 ऴ letter with nukta, Marathi/Dravidian.

U+0972 ॲ Candra अ

U+093C ़ nukta sign

Devanagari Marwari language specific Letters

U+0978 ൎ Devanagari Letter Marwari DDA

Devanagari Sindhi language specific Letters
U+097B ॻ , U+097C ॼ , U+097E ॾ , U+097F ॿ

Devanagari Limbu language specific Letters
U+097D ॽ Devanagari Letter Glottal Stop

Devanagari Konkani language specific Letters

Devanagari Bodo Dogri Maithili languages specific Letters
Latin U+02BC modified apostrophe, 093D avagraha

Devanagari Kashmiri and Bihari languages specific
U+093A ॺ , U+093B ॻ vowel signs

U+094F ॏ

U+0973 ॳ Letter oe, U+0974 ॴ Letter ooe

U+0975 ॵ Letter Candra AW

Devanagari Kashmiri language specific Mātrās
U+093A ॺ , U+093B ॻ , U+094F ॏ Vowel Sign

U+0956, U+0957,

U+0976 ॶ, U+ 0977 ॷ

Devanagari Avestan language specific Letters
U+0955 ॕ Vowel Sign

U+0979 ॹ Letter ZHA

Devanagari Sharada Lipi specific Letters
U+0900 ऀ Devanagari Sign inverted Candrabindu

Devanagari pristhmatra Mātrā (a historic glyph)
U+094E ॎ

Keyboard map for Vedic Sanskrit Typing

Normal Keyboard

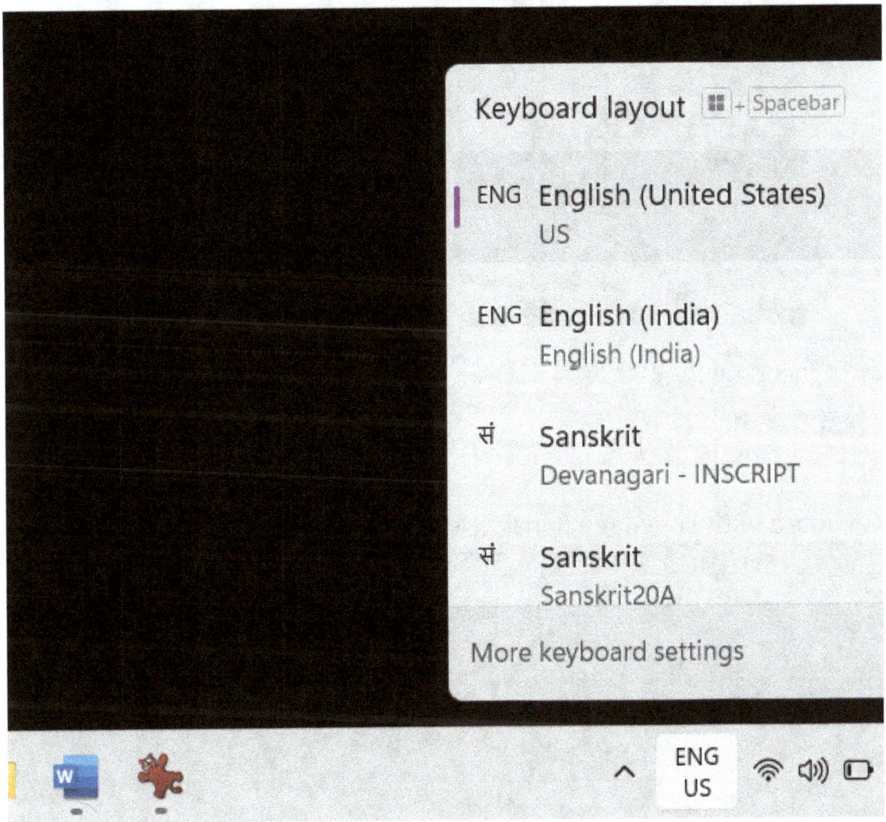

We can download this keyboard map installer file "KbdEditInstallerSANSKRIT2020A.exe" for Windows from
https://sourceforge.net/projects/advaita-sharada-font/files/Devanagari/

Unicode Block = Devanagari 0900 to 097F

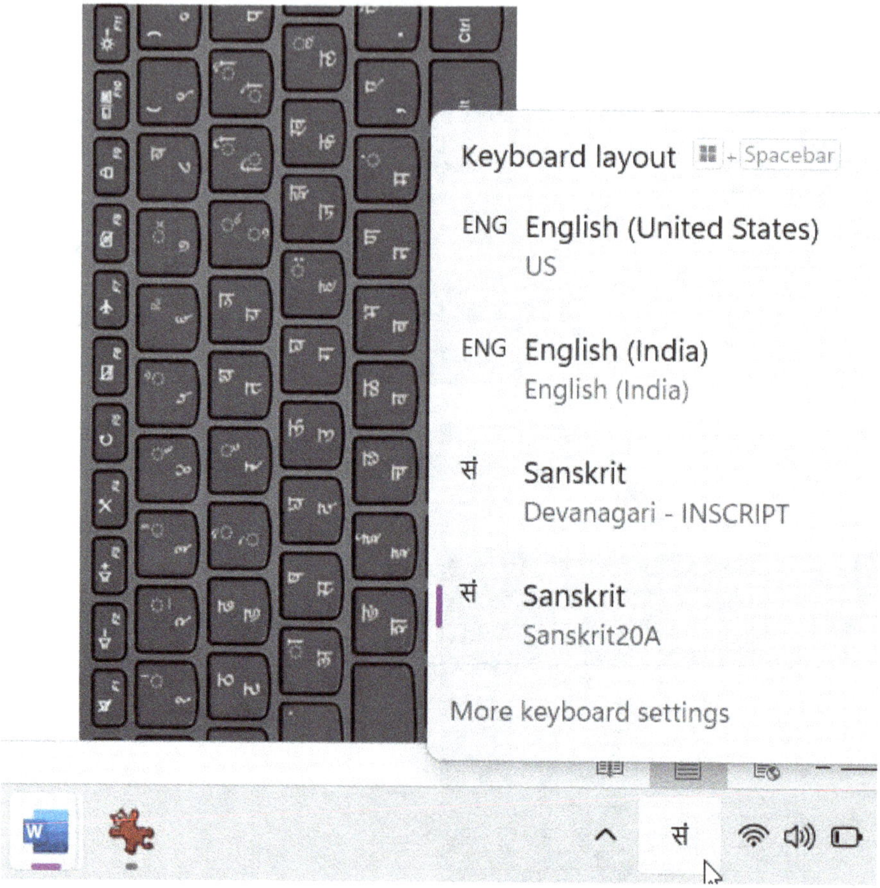

Keyboard with Language Sanskrit selected in Language bar

Use it with and without **SHIFT** key for full access to those Devanagari Unicode Block glyphs needed for Sanskrit language.

A bigger image for clarity is also given.

Unicode Block = Vedic Extensions 1CD0 to 1CFF

Keyboard with Language Sanskrit in Language bar with **PrtSc** Pressed

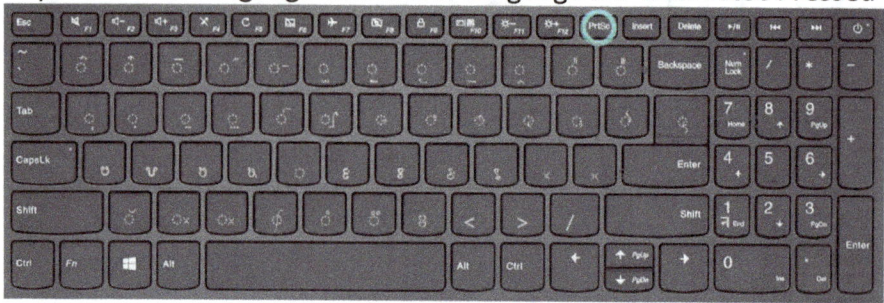

A bigger image for clarity is also given.

Unicode Block = Devanagari Extended A8E0 to A8FF

Keyboard with Language Sanskrit in Language bar with **PrtSc** Pressed. Then with **SHIFT** key press.

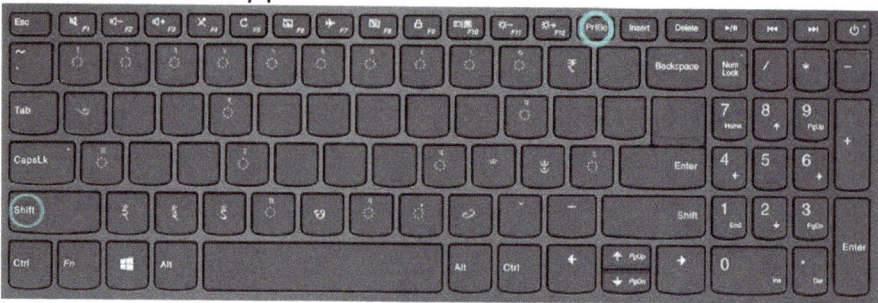

A bigger image for clarity is also given.

Open Type Design Considerations

Indic Script Devanagari

Select the Script Devanagari (deva) and Latin (latn).
Since script deva is deprecated, we may select script dev2.

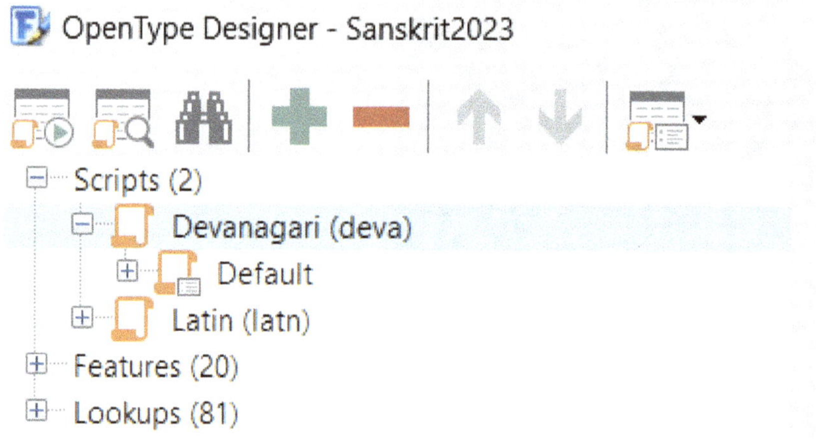

OpenType Designer - Sanskrit2023
Scripts (2)
Devanagari (deva)
Default
Latin (latn)
Features (20)
Lookups (81)

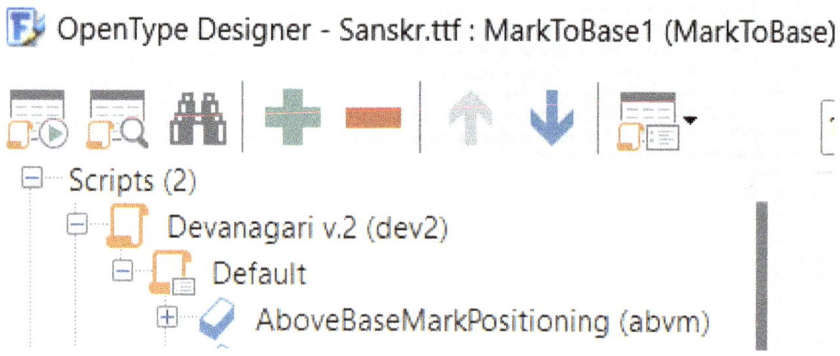

OpenType Designer - Sanskr.ttf : MarkToBase1 (MarkToBase)
Scripts (2)
Devanagari v.2 (dev2)
Default
AboveBaseMarkPositioning (abvm)

See the Shaper(s) required from an existing font.

Auto
Auto
Custom
1
_shaper
aalt
abvm
abvs
akhn
blwf
blwm
blws
cpsp
frac
half
mark
mkmk
nukt
pres
psts
rphf
sups
vatu

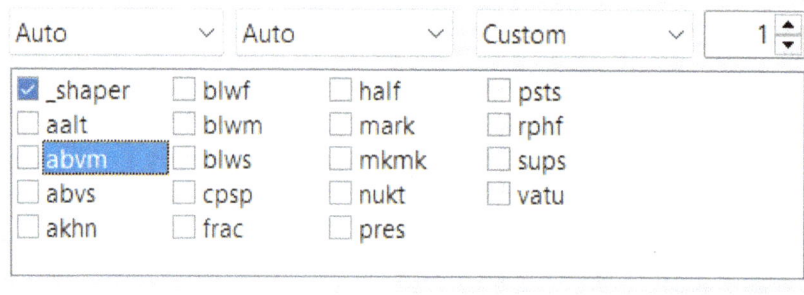

Indic Shaping Features

Add the Shaping Feature(s) required one by one.
There are two principal features in Open Type design, namely Glyph Positioning (GPOS) and Glyph Substitution (GSUB). Each feature has some shaping code lookups, which we can add during Font Design.

```
Add Lookup

Devanagari v.2 (dev2) -> Default -> AboveBaseMarkPositioning (abvm)

Lookup
  ○ Existing lookup     ChainedContextPositioning1

  Glyph Positioning (GPOS)              Glyph Substitution (GSUB)
  ● Single adjustment                   ○ Single substitution
  ○ Pair adjustment                     ○ Multiple substitution (decompose)
  ○ Cursive attachment                  ○ Alternate substitution
  ○ Mark to base attachment             ○ Ligature substitution
  ○ Mark to ligature attachment         ○ Chained context substitution
  ○ Mark to mark attachment             ○ Reverse chaining context substitution
  ○ Chained context positioning
```

AboveBaseMarkPositioning (abvm)
> MarkToBase-attaching anchor of mark glyph with base glyph, e.g. U0915+0902 क ं precise positioning of Mark.

AboveBaseSubstitutions (abvs)
> Ligature-replacing overlapping glyphs with new drawn ligature glyphs ी ी that do not overlap.

Akhands (akhn)
> Ligature-replacing क + ् + ष combination glyphs with new drawn ligature क्ष glyph

BelowBaseForms (blwf)
> ChainingContext- क ् → क्

BelowBaseMarkPositioning (blwm)

MarkToBase-attaching anchor of mark glyph with base glyph
MarkToMark-attaching anchor of mark glyph with mark glyph

BelowBaseSubstitutions (blws)
: Ligature-replacing overlapping glyphs with new drawn smaller glyphs that do not overlap.

ConjunctForms (cjct)
: Ligature-replacing consonant glyph combinations, with new drawn ligature glyph, as seen in Sanskrit literature.

HalantForms (haln)
: Ligature-replacing glyphs where halant intersects, with new drawn glyph where halant is well positioned.

HalfForms (half)
: Ligature-replacing consonant+halant glyphs with new drawn half-consonant glyph.

NuktaForms (nukt)
: Ligature-replacing the combination of consonant+nukta glyphs with a new ligature.

PostBaseSubstitutions (psts)
: Ligature-replacing the combination of consonant+halant glyphs with a new ligature.

PreBaseSubstitutions (pres)
: Ligature-replacing the combination of consonant+halant+consonant glyphs with a new ligature.

RakarForms (rkrf)
: Ligature-replacing consonant+halant+repha combination glyphs with new drawn Ligature conjunct having back slash for repha

RephForms (rphf)
: Ligature-for replacing repha+halant glyphs with top curve glyph

VattuVariants (vatu)
: Ligature-replacing consonant+halant+repha combination glyphs with new Ligature conjunct with caret below for repha

Adding a Feature for the Shaping Engine.

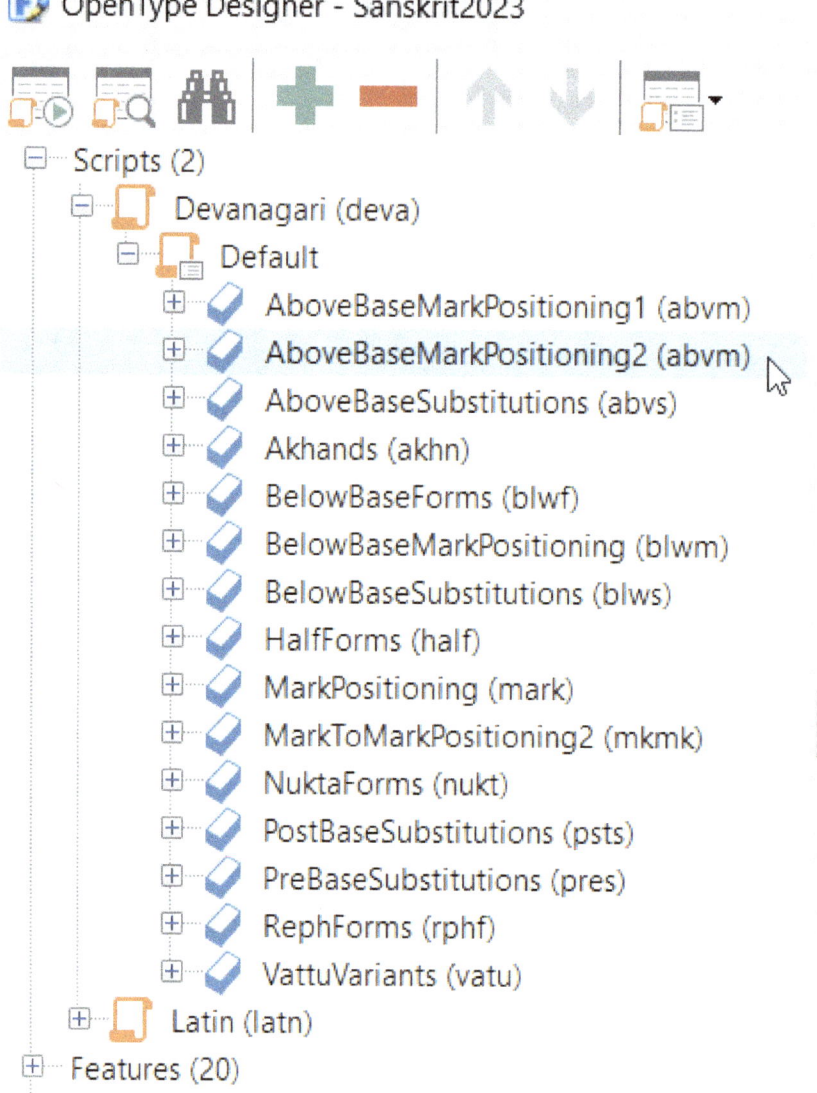

Principal Features needed for a Devanagari Font.

AboveBaseMarkPositioning (abvm)

Feature = MarkToBase
MarkToBase - Attaching anchor of such a mark glyph that must be attached above the base glyph. This works for **two independent glyphs**, and is used to adjust the relative position of both such that the final glyph is correct as per the Sanskrit literature.

It uses Anchors that shall be adjusted for positioning. One glyph has attribute **base glyph**, and the other glyph has attribute **mark glyph**. Then we use the **MarkToBase** feature.

Used for attaching marks like Anusvara, Candrabindu, Svarita (Udatta) to the Vowels and Consonants-with-inherent-vowel.

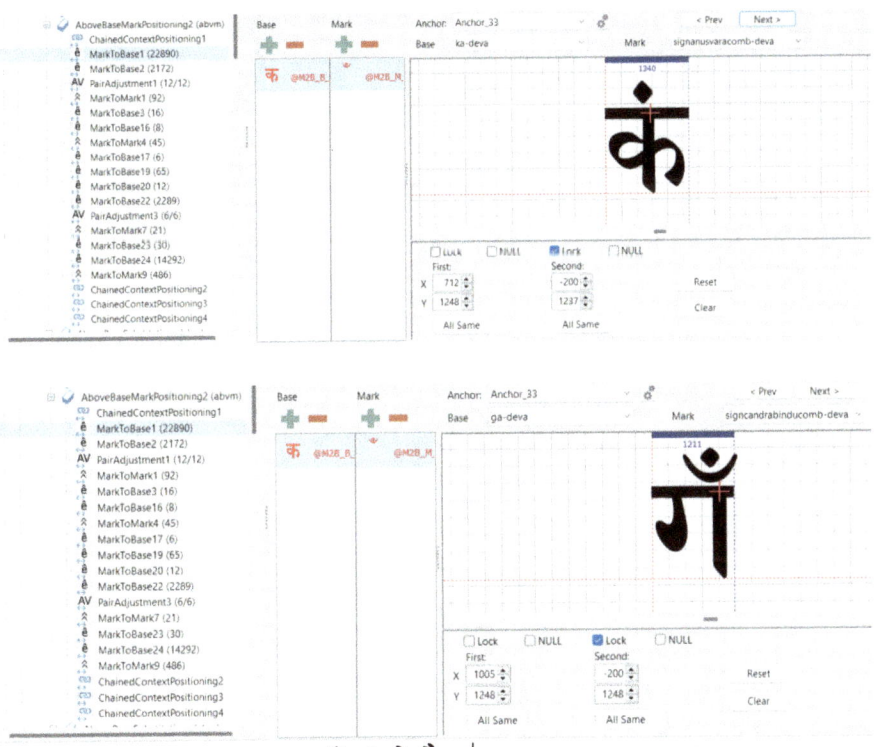

Above mark glyphs array ӑ ӓ ӓ ӑ Devanagari Block.
Above mark glyphs array ӑ ӑ ӑ ӑ ӑ ӑ° VedicExtensions Block.

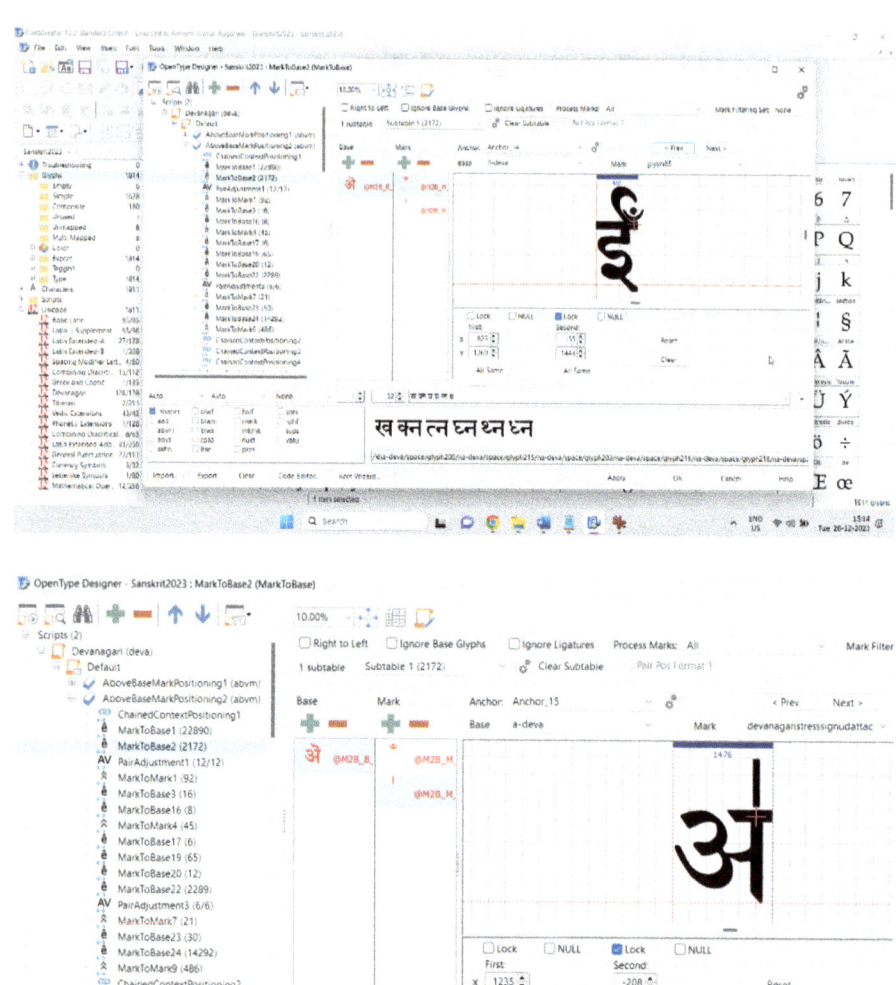

Firstly, we need to specify the dotted circle glyph for all above base marks, that should be inserted in case a required base glyph is absent.

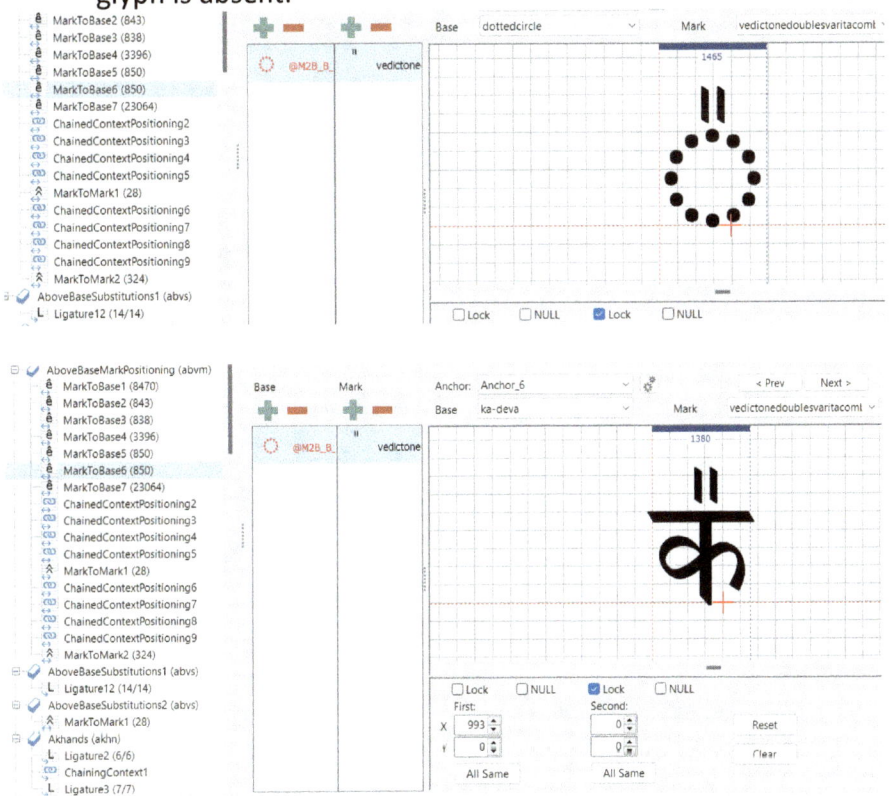

Feature = PairAdjustment

PairAdjustment – Adjusting the precise position of two mark glyphs wrt each other.

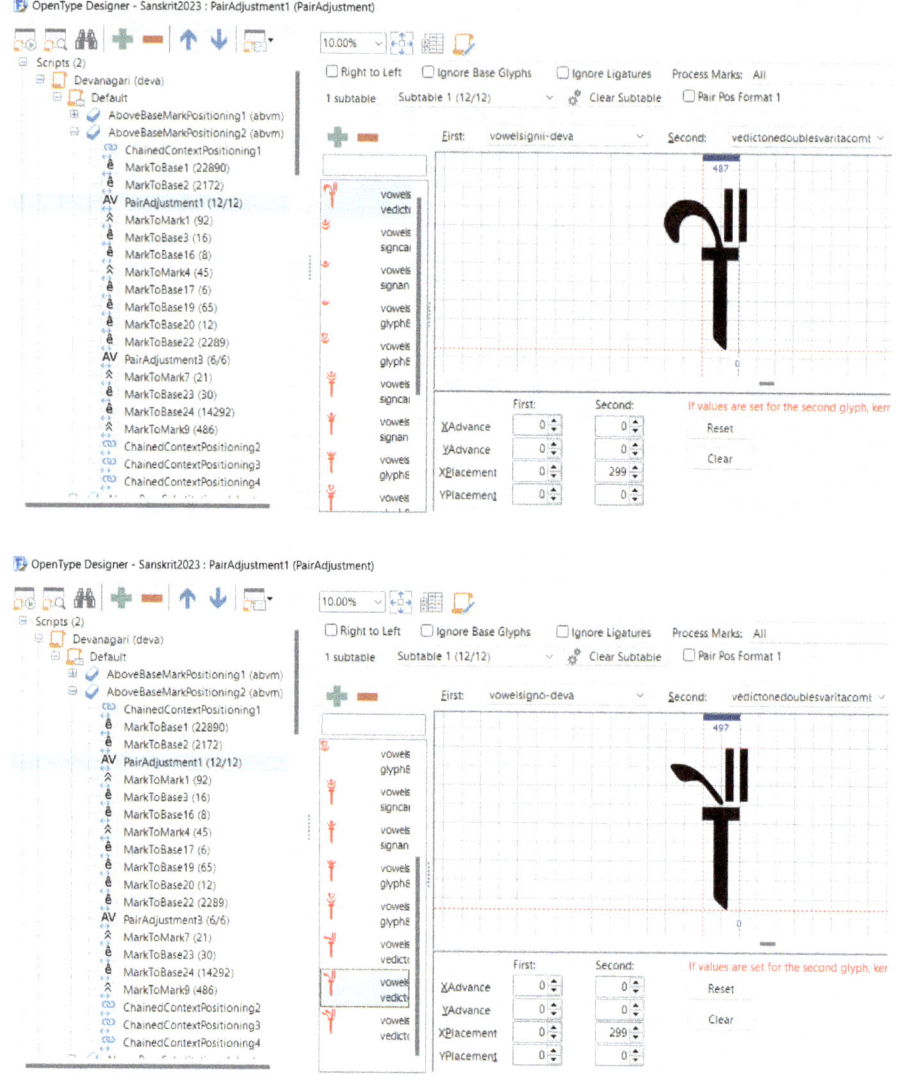

Question: Should we use MarkToMark here?

What actually works? MarkToMark or PairAdjustment?

The fonts SanskritText and AdobeDevanagari do not use PairAdjustment feature here. MarkToMark is used.

Feature = MarkToMark
MarkToMark – Adjusting the precise position of two mark glyphs wrt each other.

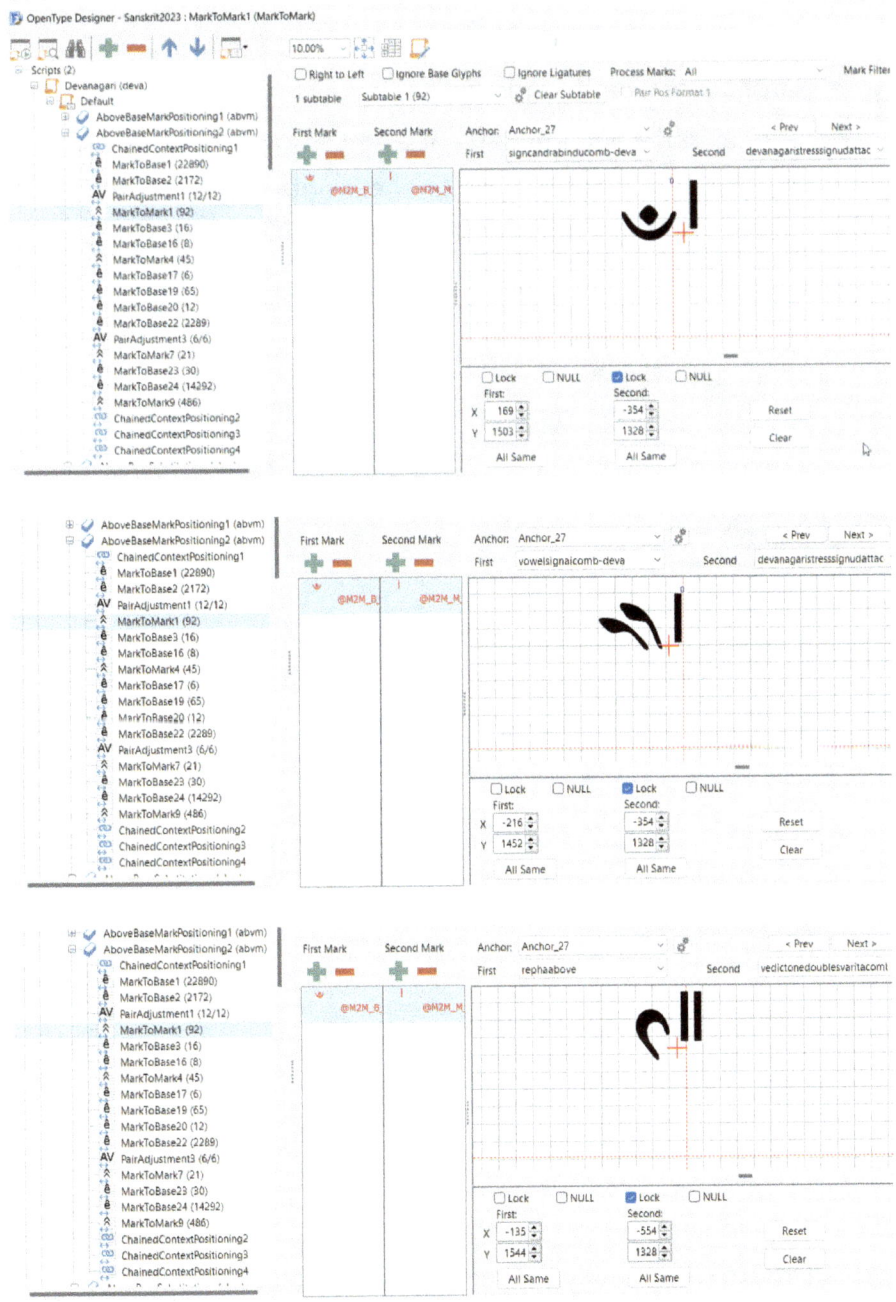

Feature = MarkToBase

MarkToBase – Adjusting the precise position of

- Visarga and Svarita कः
- Visarga and Anudatta कः
- Ardhavisarga and Svarita कᳵ
- Ardhavisarga and Anudatta कᳵ

wrt each other. This helps to position the Svarita to the top of the Letter and not above Visarga. Similarly Anudatta below Letter.

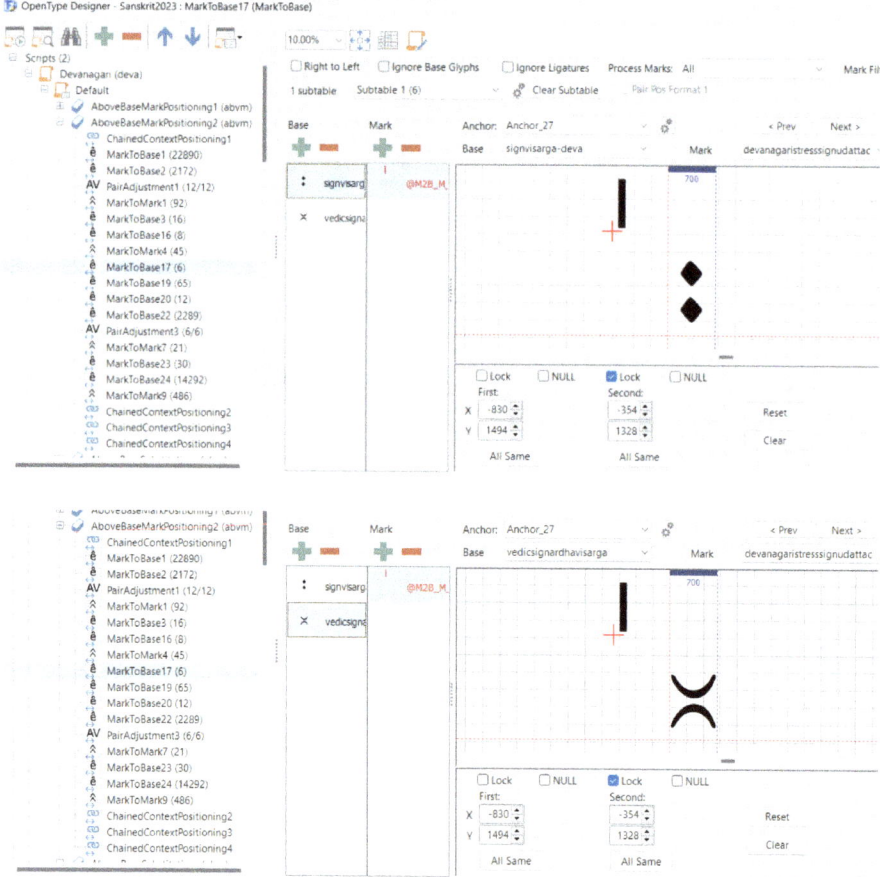

Note: The Indic Shaping properties for ardhavisarga are missing. To be implemented by the Shaping Engine or by Microsoft Word.

Note: As a workaround, we see that it gets typed correctly कᳵ when we use Insert Symbol to type Svarita (and not directly from keyboard). Similarly कᳵ

Feature = MarkToBase
MarkToBase – Adjusting the placement of glyphs from the Devanagari Extended block.

- Vowel and combining numeral अ॒

- Vowel and combining letter अ ओ

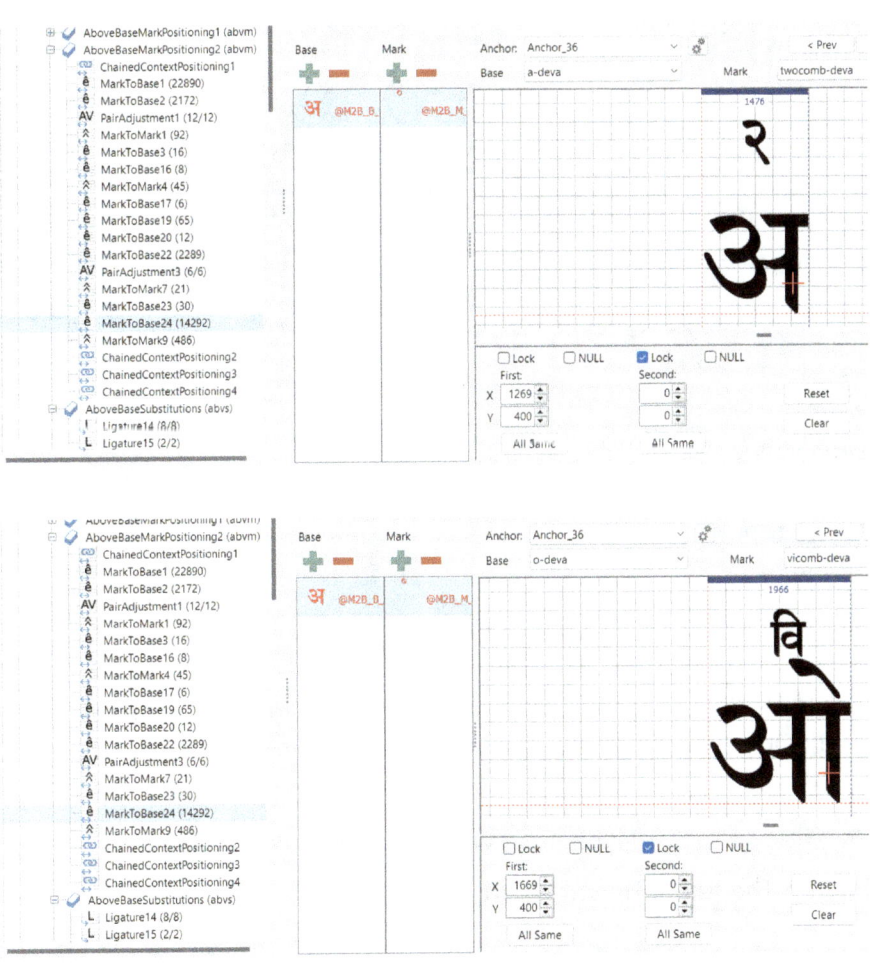

Feature = ChainedContextPositioning
ChainedContextPositioning – Adjusting the placement of three glyphs wrt each other.

- RephaHalant Letter Matra रू क ि → र्कि

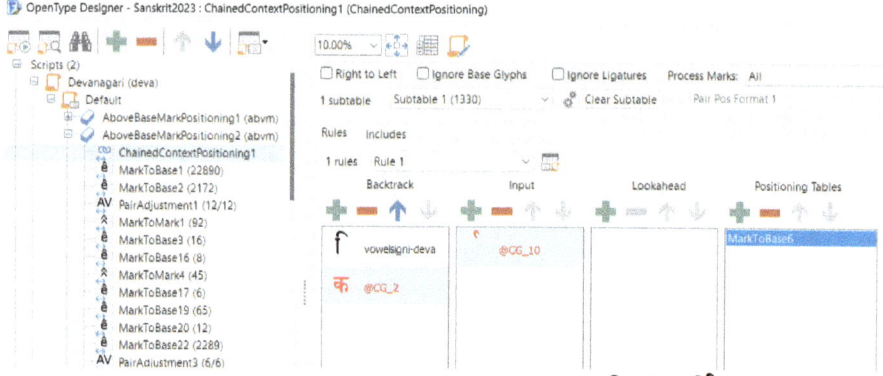

- RephaHalant Letter Matra Anusvara रू क ि ं → र्किं

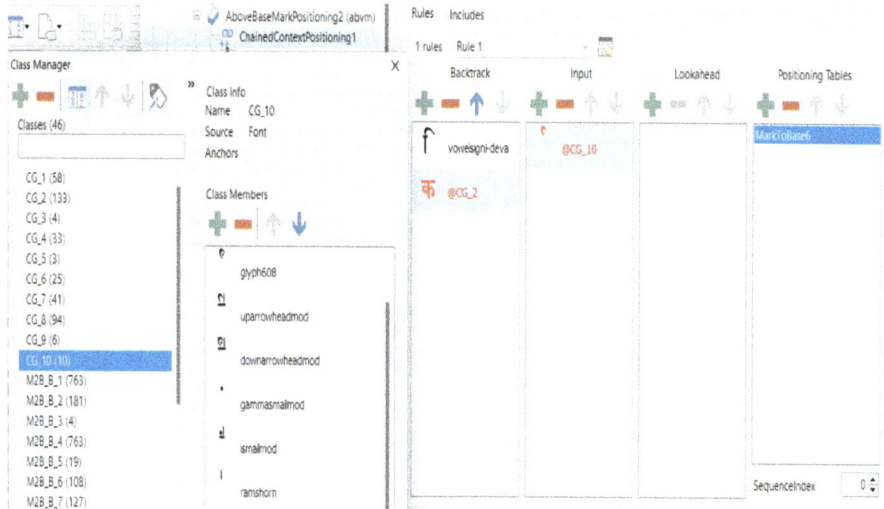

Class Manager for grouping glyphs with same Indic Shaping rules.
Note: Only three glyphs are in operation in this Feature, viz.

Backtrack = Matra glyph ि

Backtrack = Letter glyph क on which Matra shall attach

Input = The RephaHalant glyph

We use a Class Manager to group glyphs with similar operations.
Here CG_2 = array of glyphs (क ख ग घ etc.)
Here CG_10 = array of glyphs (ि ी etc.)

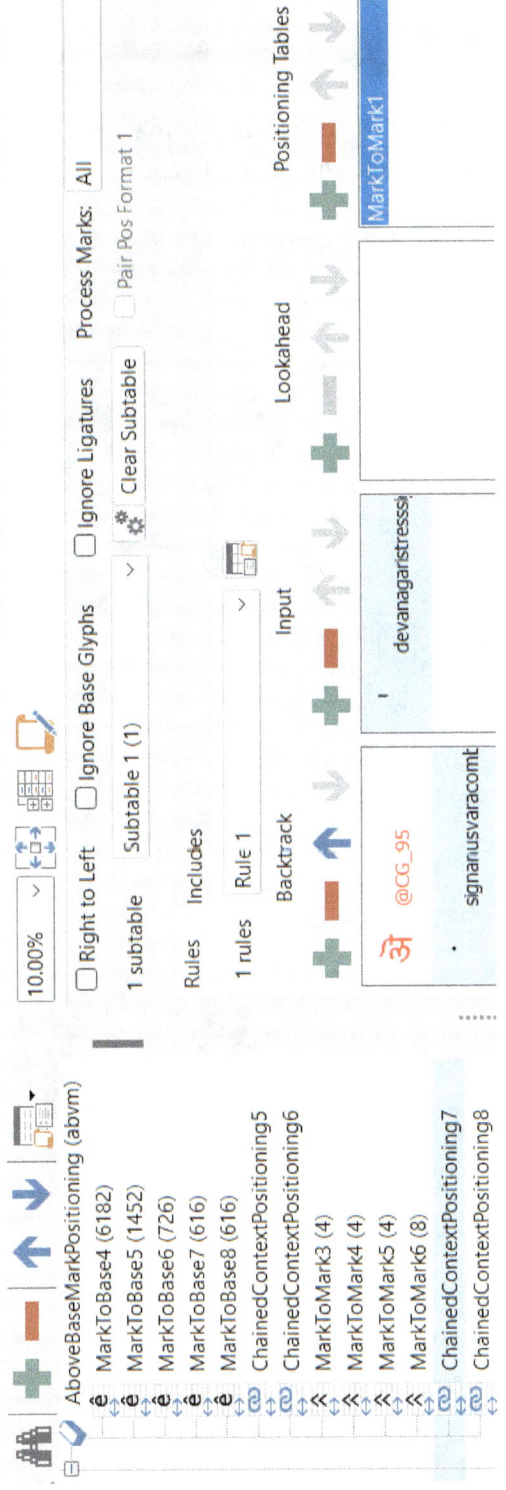

AboveBaseSubstitutions (abvs)

Feature = Ligature.

For replacing the combination of rephaHalant+matra glyphs with a new ligature. Otherwise it will be incorrectly positioned due to overlap.

E.g. rephaHalant+consonant+matra रूक ी → कीं

ीं ीं are new drawn Ligatures.

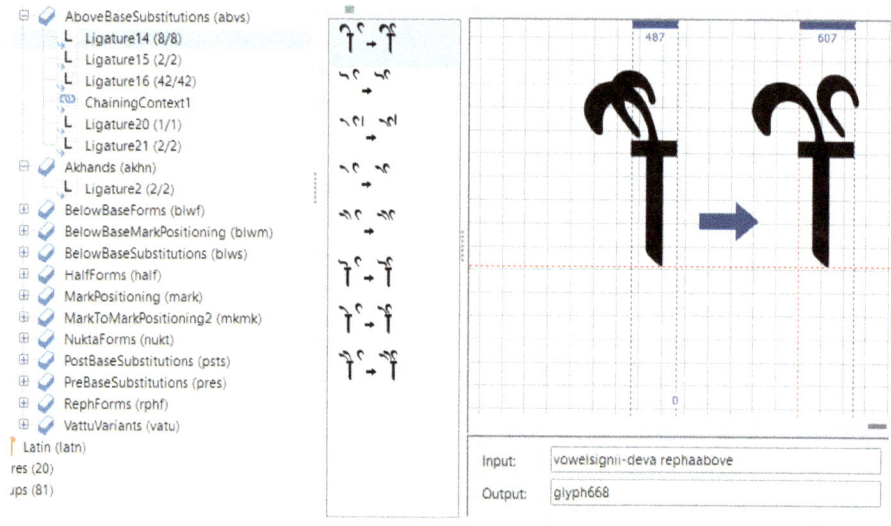

E.g. rephaHalant+vowel+candrabindu रूई ँ → ईं

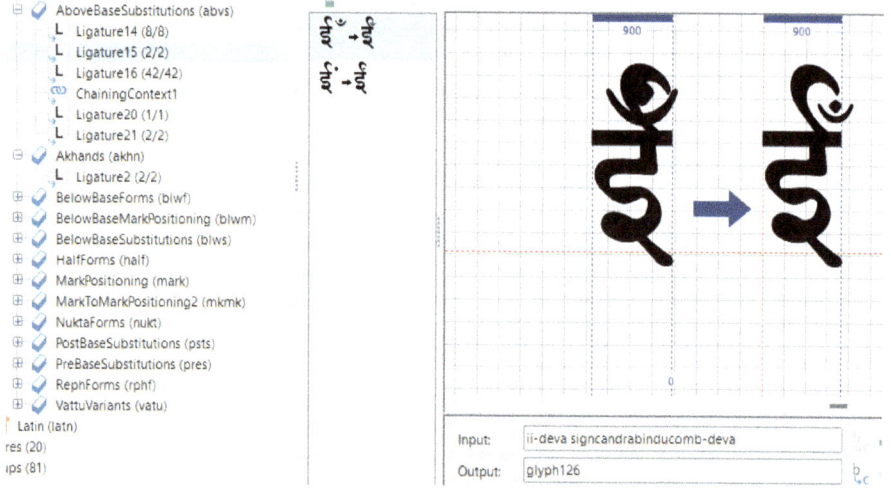

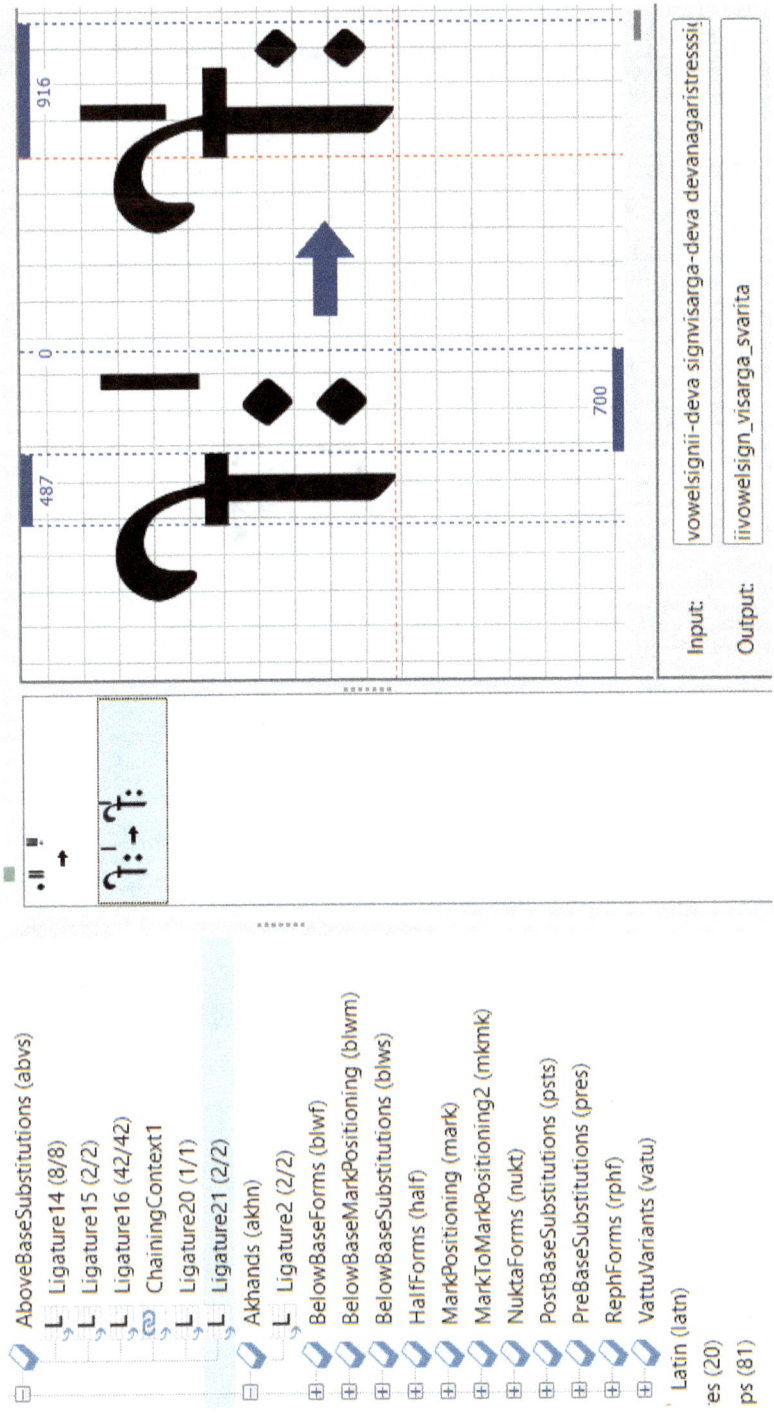

E.g. consonant+matra+visarga+svarita क ी ः ॑ → कीः॑

65

Akhands (akhn)

Feature = Ligature.
For replacing the combination of consonant+halant+consonant glyphs with a new ligature. Used only for two ligatures called akhands, namely

क् ष → क्ष where क्ष is a new Ligature.

ज् ञ → ज्ञ where ज्ञ is a new Ligature.

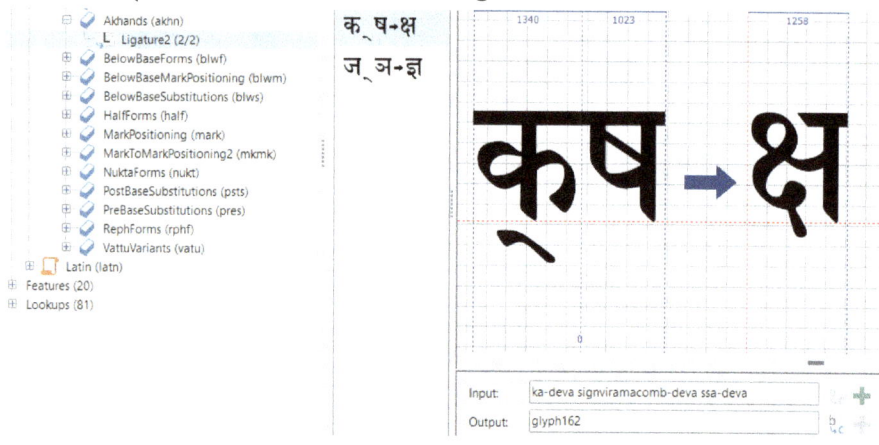

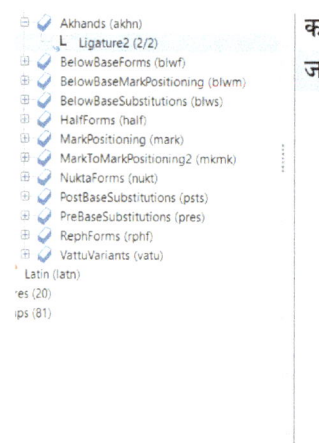
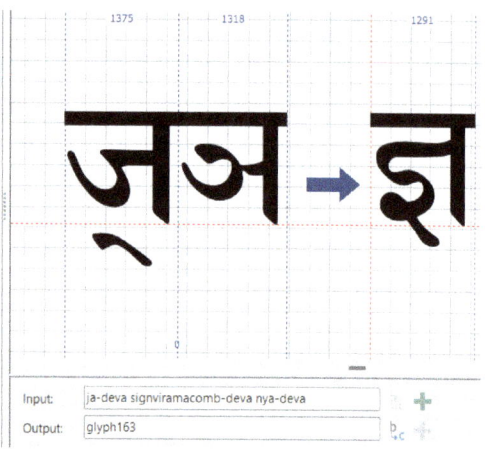

BelowBaseForms (blwf)

Feature = ChainingContext.
For replacing the combination of consonant+halant glyphs with a new ligature. E.g. क् → क्

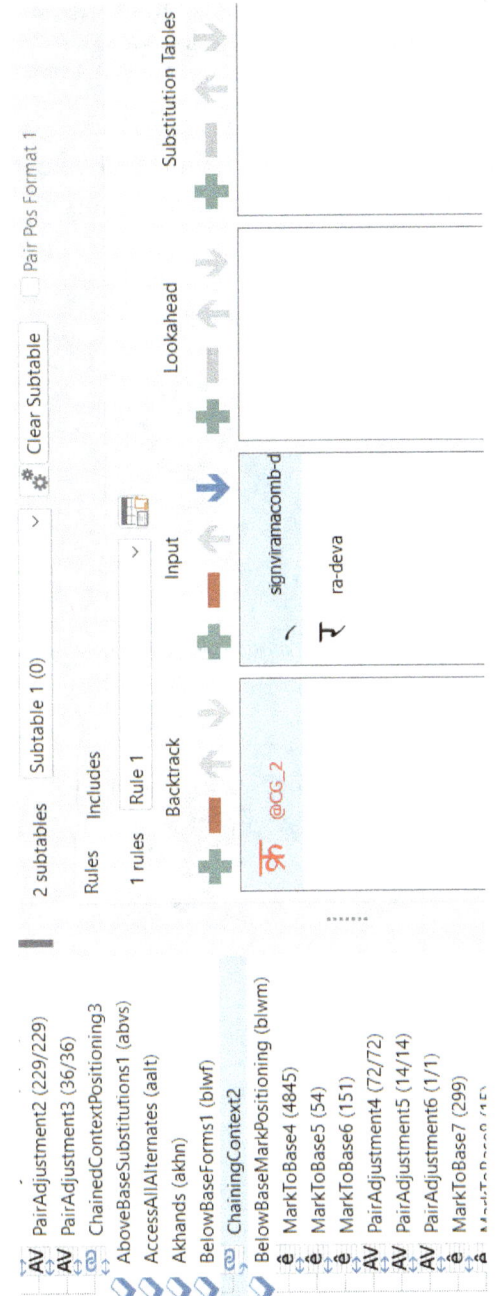

67

BelowBaseMarkPositioning (blwm)

Feature = MarkToBase

MarkToBase - Attaching anchor of such a mark glyph that must be attached below the base glyph. This works for **two independent glyphs**, and is used to adjust the relative position of both such that the final glyph is correct as per the Sanskrit literature.

Firstly, we need to specify the dotted circle glyph for all below base marks, that should be inserted in case a required base glyph is absent.

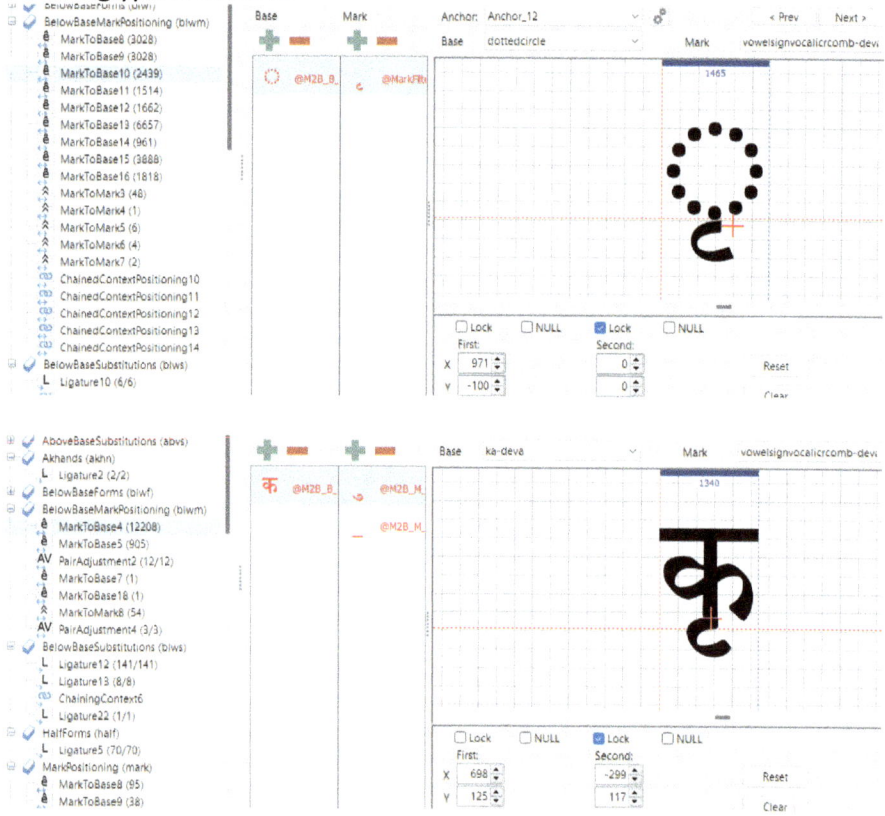

Below mark glyphs array ◌ँ ◌ं ◌ः ◌ऺ ◌ऻ ◌ॅ ◌ॆ Devanagari Block.
Below mark glyphs array ◌ॖ ◌ॗ ◌ॢ ◌ॣ ◌ॱ ◌ॲ ◌ॳ ◌ॴ ◌ॵ VedicExtensions.

Feature = MarkToMark

MarkToMark - Adjusting the precise position of two mark glyphs wrt each other that are placed below a base glyph.

e.g. Letter+uMatra+anudattaAccent

All three glyphs are from Devanagari block. क ु ॒ → कु॒

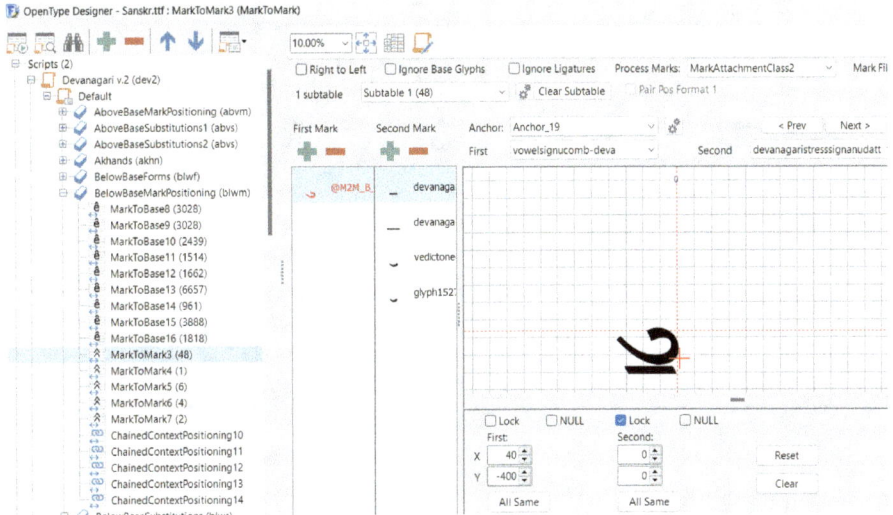

Glyphs are from Devanagari and VedicExtensions. क ॒ ू → कू॒

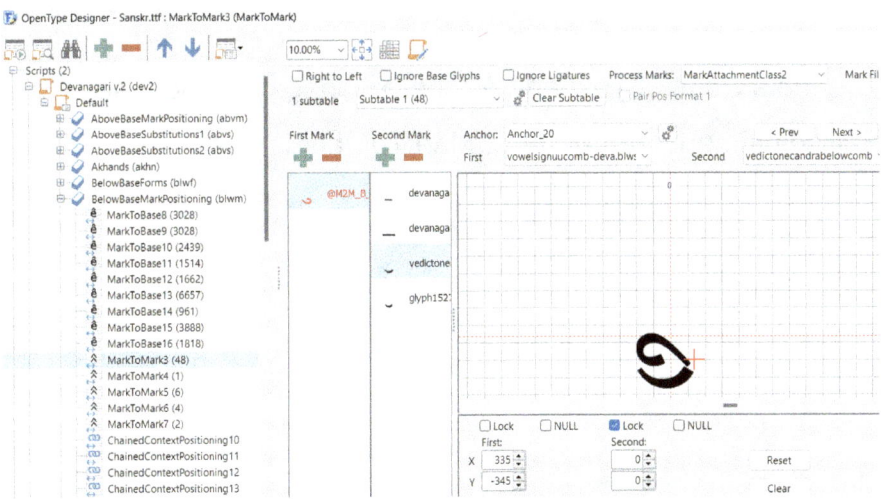

Feature = PairAdjustment

PairAdjustment - Adjusting the precise position of two mark glyphs wrt each other that are placed below a base glyph.

e.g. Letter+uMatra+anudattaAccent

All three glyphs are from Devanagari block. क ु ॒ → कु॒

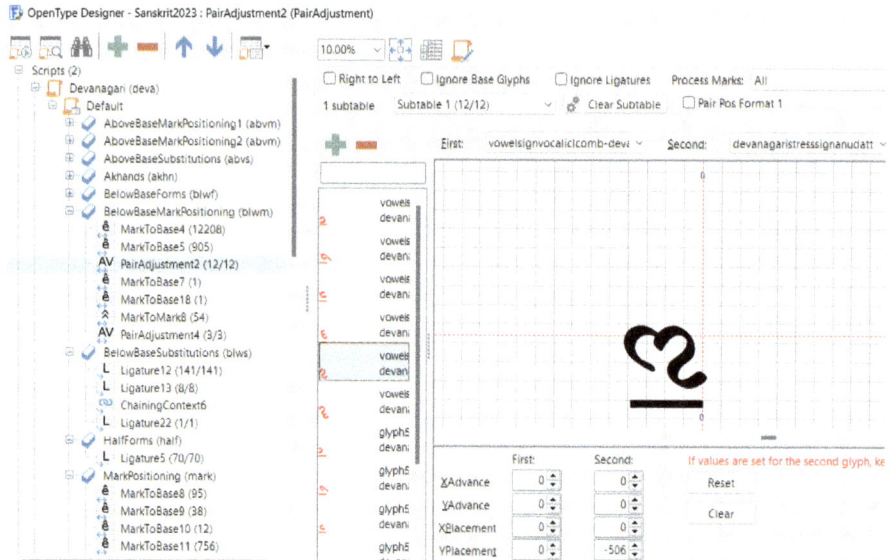

Question: Should we use MarkToMark here?

What actually works? MarkToMark or PairAdjustment?

The fonts SanskritText and AdobeDevanagari do not use PairAdjustment feature here. MarkToMark is used.

Feature = MarkToBase

MarkToBase - Attaching anchor of such a mark glyph that must be attached below the base glyph. This works for **two independent glyphs**, and is used to adjust the relative position of both such that the final glyph is correct as per the Sanskrit literature.

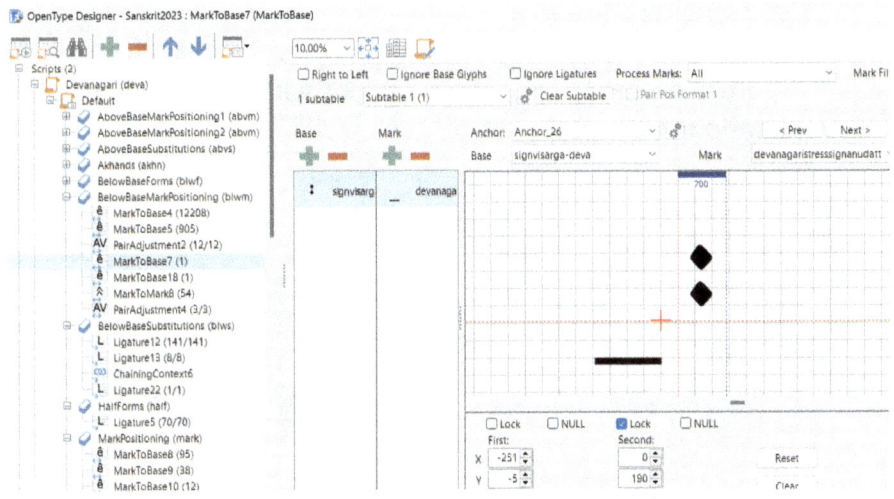

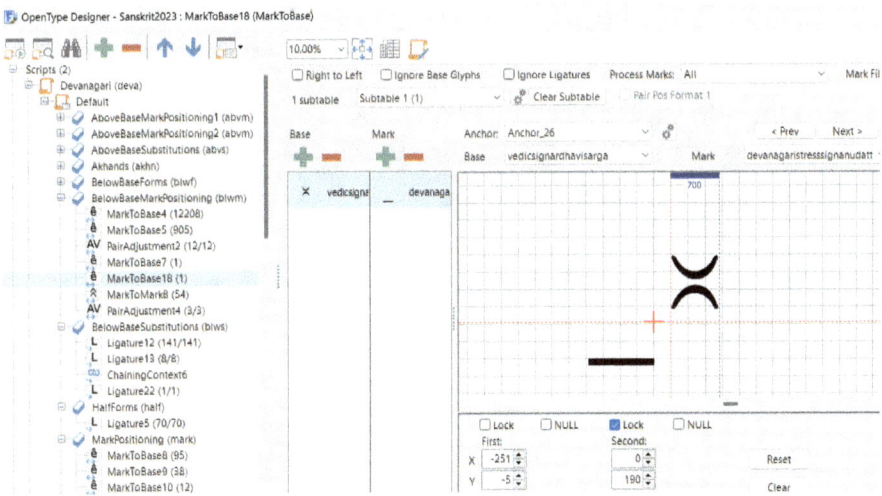

Proposal: Ardhavisarga needs to be implemented for it to work.

Question: Should we use MarkToMark here?

BelowBaseSubstitutions (blws)

Feature = Ligature

Ligature - Attaching anchor of such a mark glyph that must be attached below the base glyph. This works for **two independent glyphs**, and is used to adjust the relative position of both such that the final glyph is correct as per the Sanskrit literature.

Ligature-replacing overlapping glyphs with new drawn glyph that do not overlap.

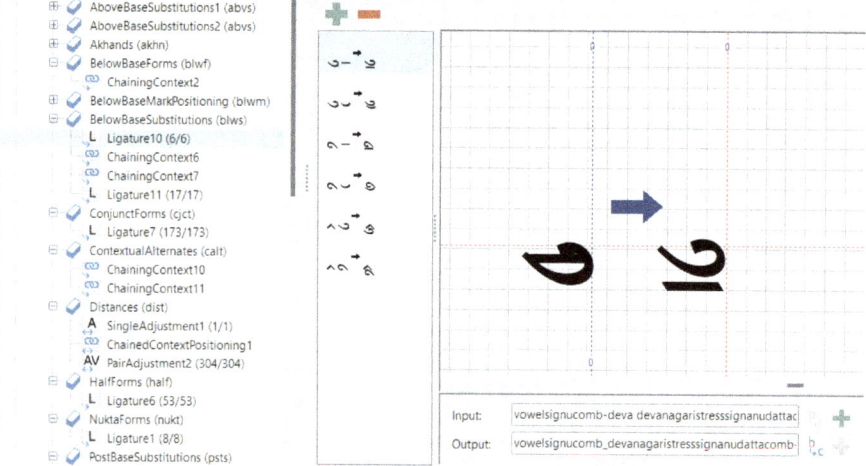

Question: SanskritText font uses both blwm and blws in this present case? Why? BelowBaseMarkPositioning with feature MarkToMark / BelowBaseSubstitutions with feature Ligature.

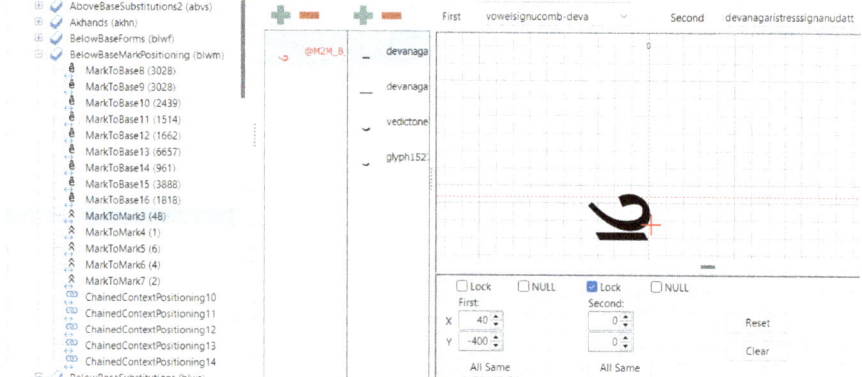

Note: AdobeDevanagari font uses only blwm in this present case.

ट ः ः → टु ( Sanskrit2023 needs rectification)

BelowBaseMarkPositioning with feature MarkToMark.

But for this case it uses the BelowBaseSubstitutions with feature Ligature.

ट ः र ः → टृ

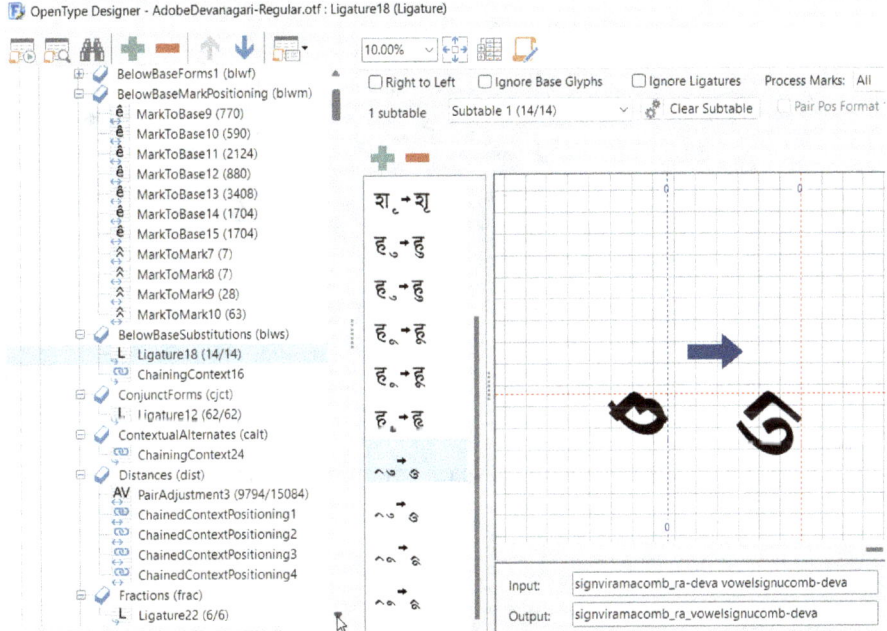

टृ टृ टृ Annapurna SIL टृ

Feature = Ligature.
For replacing the combination of repha+uMatra glyphs with a new ligature.

E.g. र ु → रु

र ू → रू

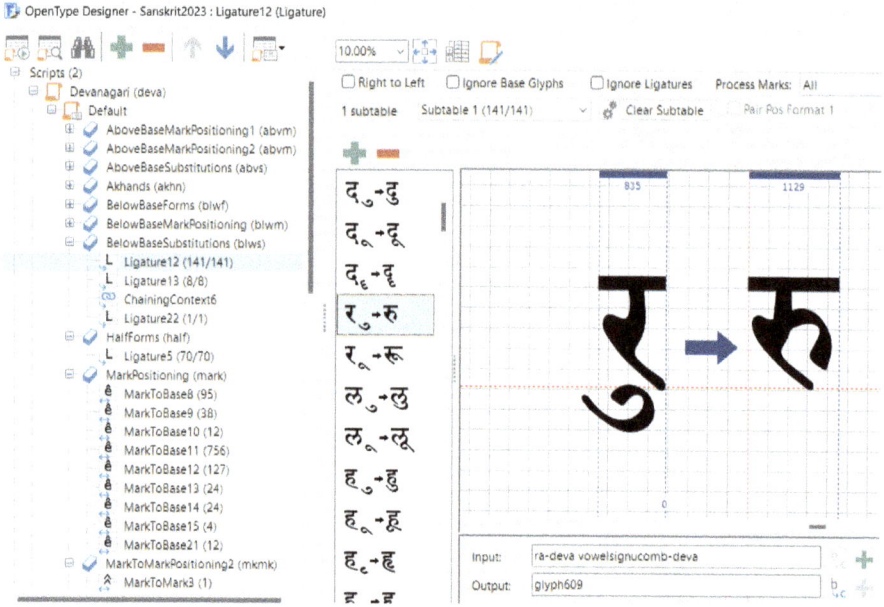

Also other glyphs where neatness or specific ligature is desired.

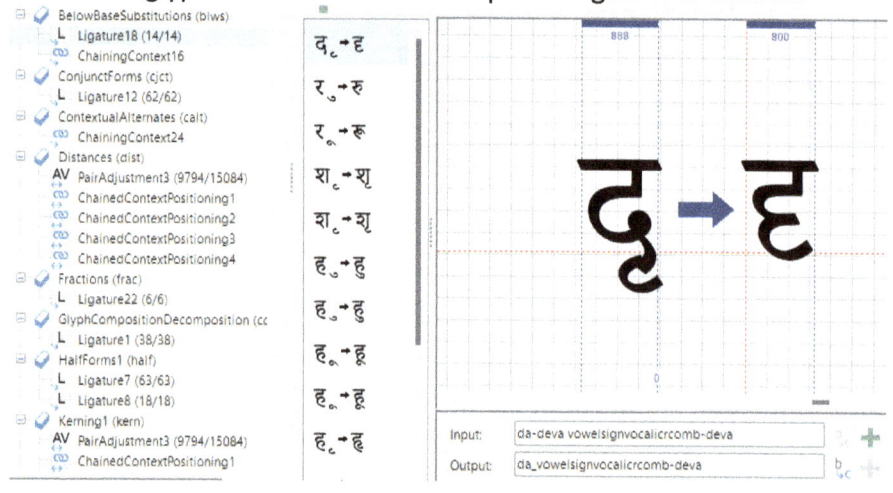

ConjunctForms (cjct)

Feature = Ligature.

For replacing the combination of consonant+halant+consonant glyphs with a new conjunct ligature found in literature.

E.g. क ् क → क्क where क्क is a new Ligature.

ङ ् क → ङ्क where ङ्क is a new Ligature.

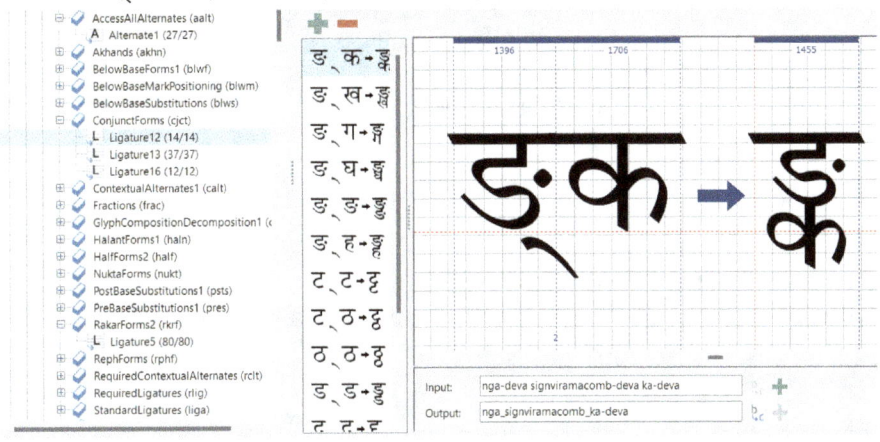

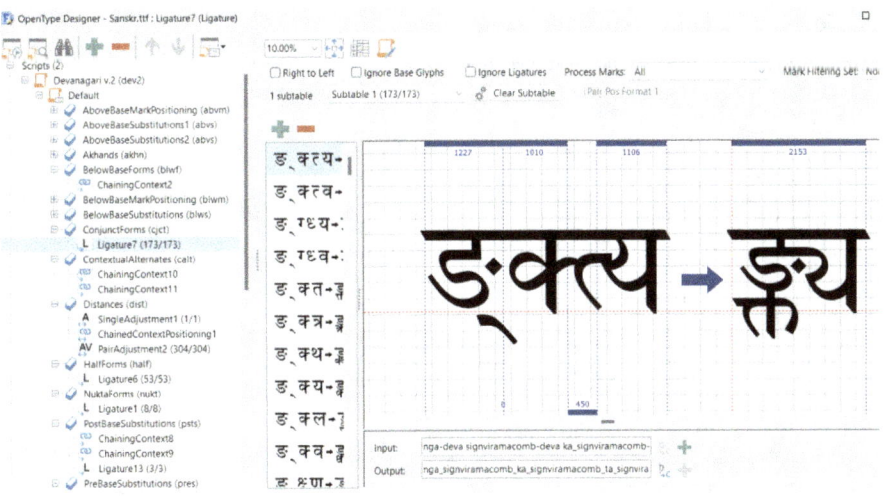

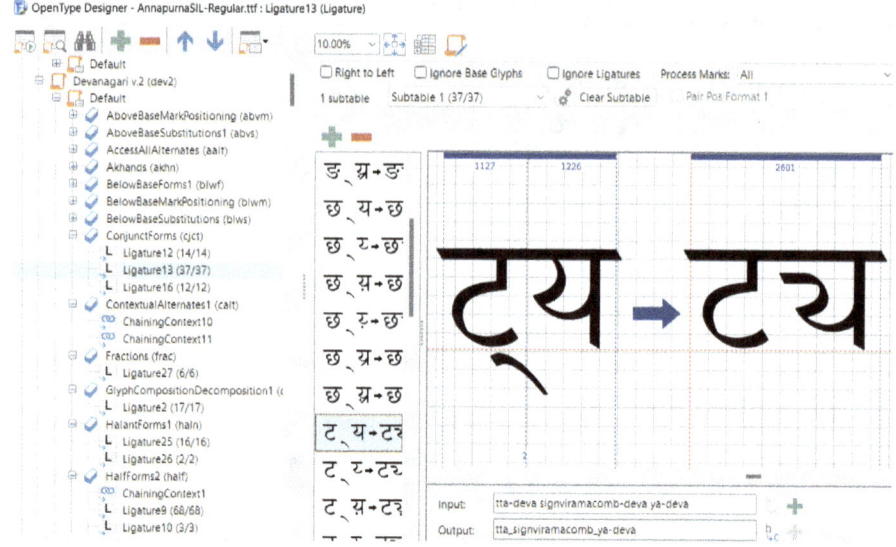

Feature = ChainingContext.
For replacing the combination of glyphs with a new ligature.

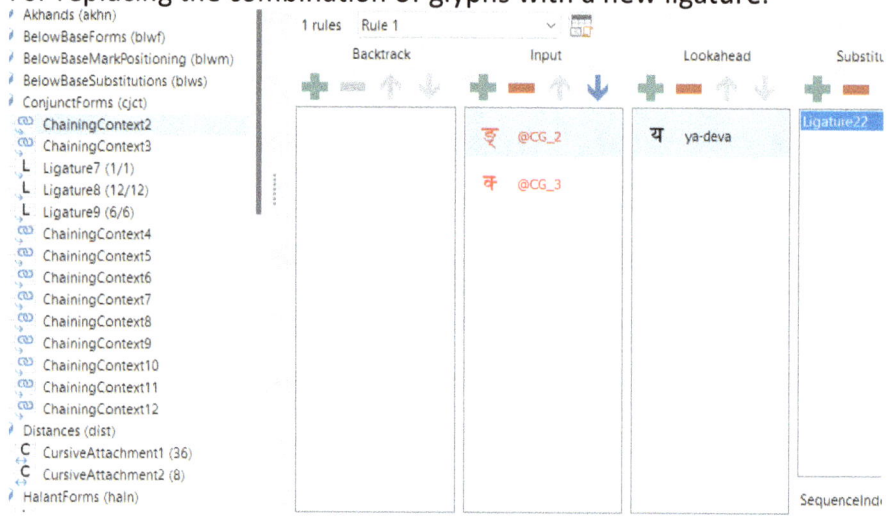

HalantForms (haln)

Feature = Ligature.

For replacing the combination of consonant+halant glyphs with a new ligature where halant is well positioned.

E.g. द ् → द् where द् is a new Ligature.

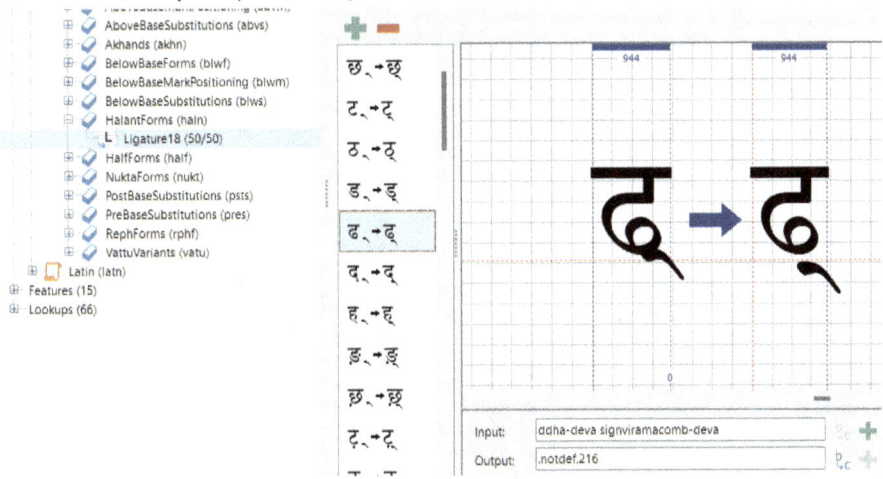

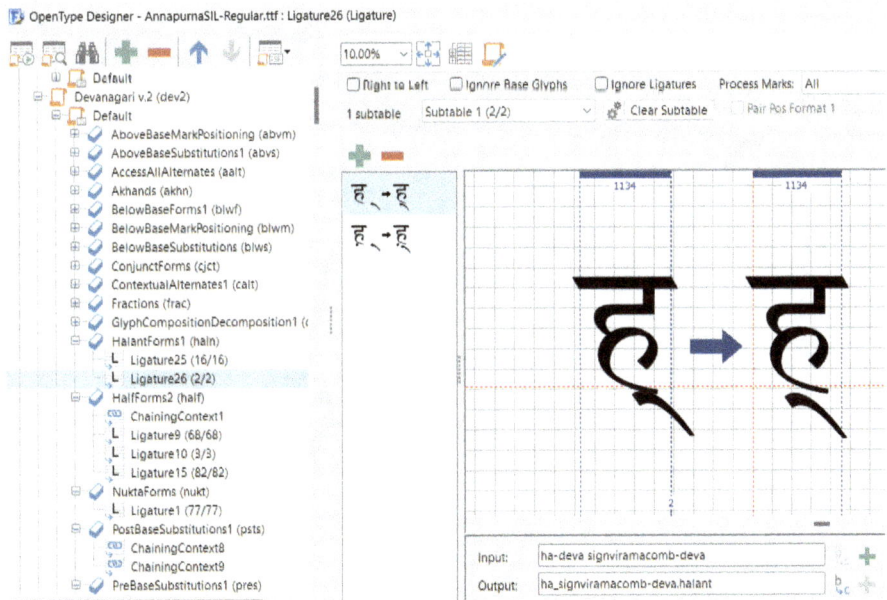

HalfForms (half)

Feature = Ligature.

For replacing the combination of consonant+halant glyphs with a new half-consonant ligature.

E.g. क ् → क्‍ where क्‍ is a new Ligature.

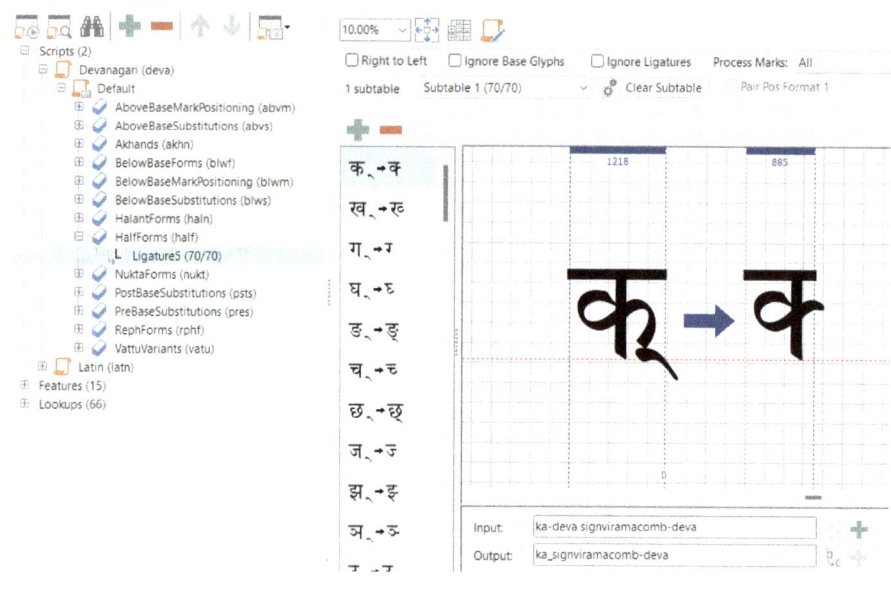

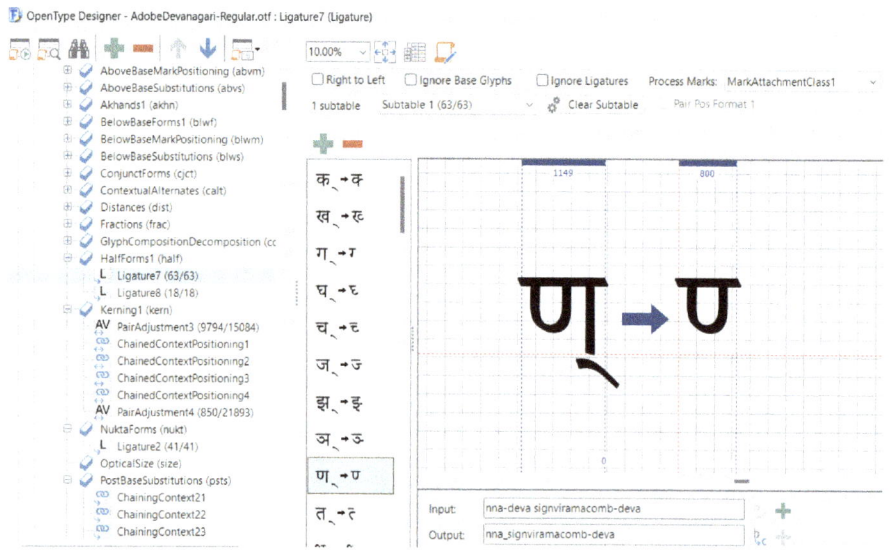

MarkPositioning (mark)

MarkToMarkPositioning (mkmk)

https://learn.microsoft.com/en-us/typography/opentype/spec/features_ko

NuktaForms (nukt)

Feature = Ligature.
For replacing the combination of consonant+nukta glyphs with a new ligature.

E.g. ज ़ → ज़ where ज़ is a new Ligature with nukta correctly placed. Used only for Consonants क ख ग ज ड ढ फ य र ळ

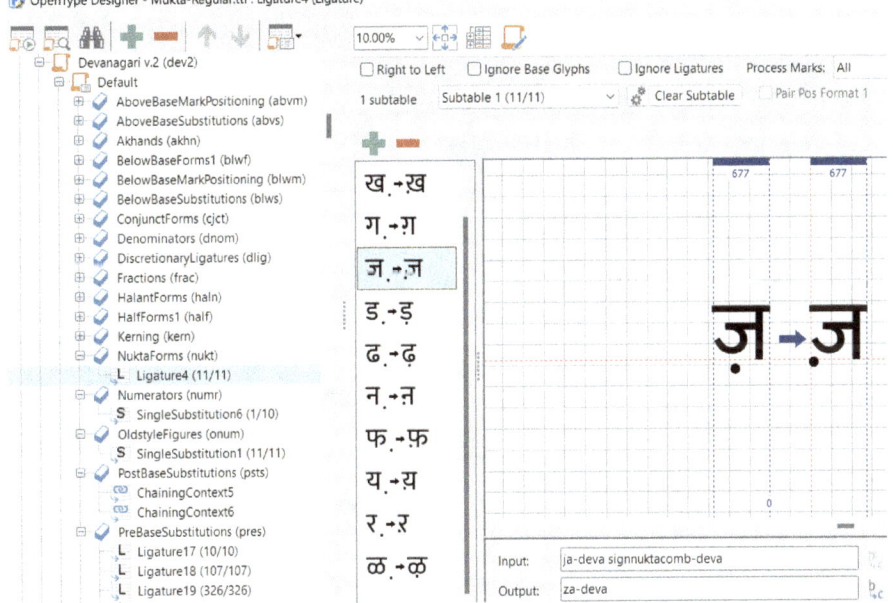

PostBaseSubstitutions (psts)

Feature = Ligature.
For replacing the combination of consonant+halant glyphs with a new ligature.

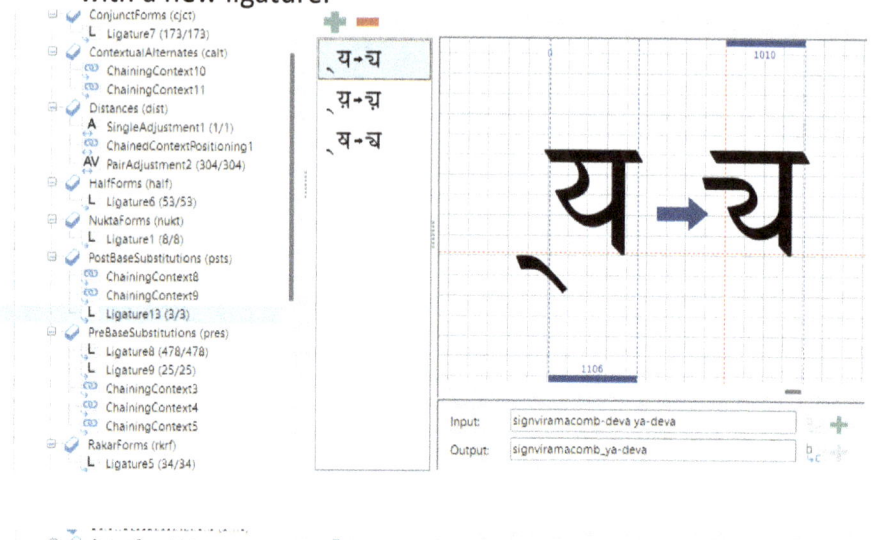

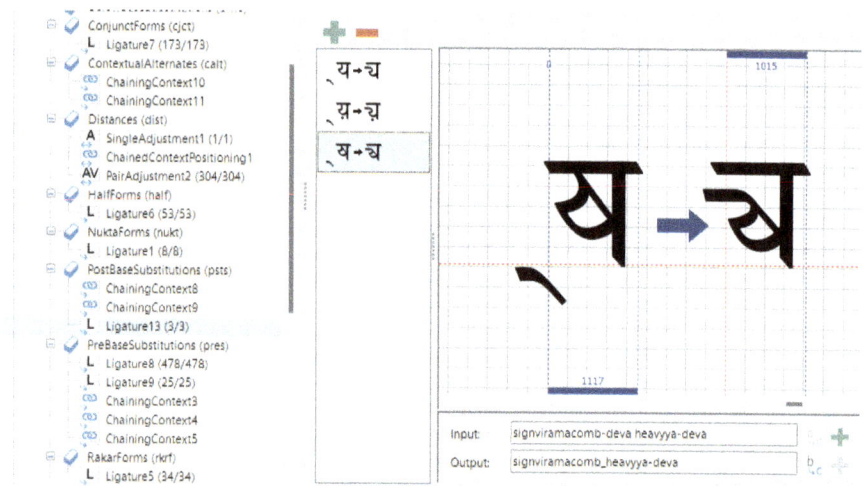

This feature replaces post-base-consonant glyphs with special ligatures. E.g. stylistic variants of right-side matra.

फ ी → फी → फी

Feature = ChainingContext.
For replacing the combination of consonant+iMatra glyphs with a new ligature having correctly shaped iMatra.

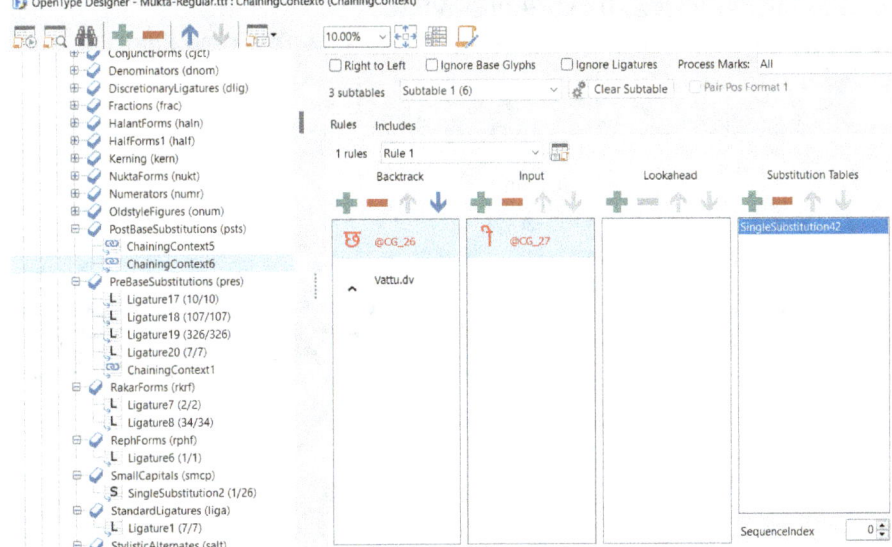

PreBaseSubstitutions (pres)

Feature = Ligature.
For replacing the combination of consonant+halant+consonant glyphs with a new ligature.

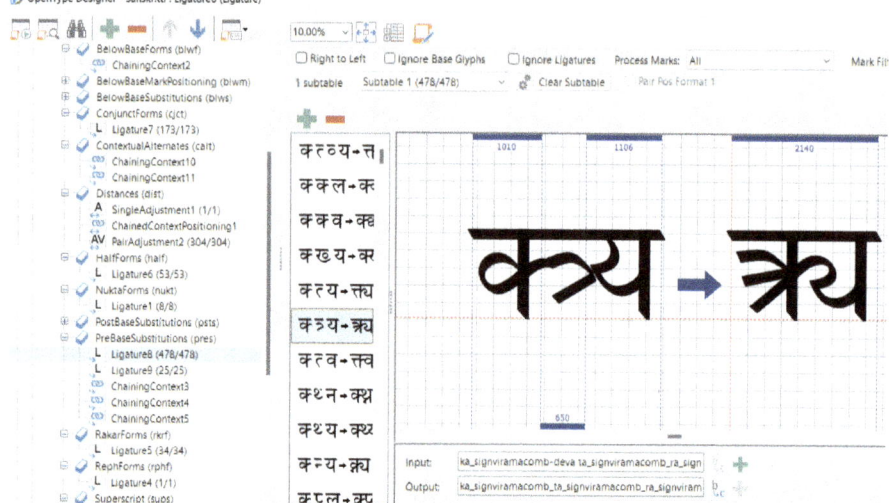

This feature replaces pre-base-consonant glyphs with special ligatures. E.g. stylistic variants of left-side matra.

ख ि → खि → खि

Feature = ChainingContext.
For replacing the combination of consonant+iMatra glyphs with a new ligature having correctly shaped iMatra.

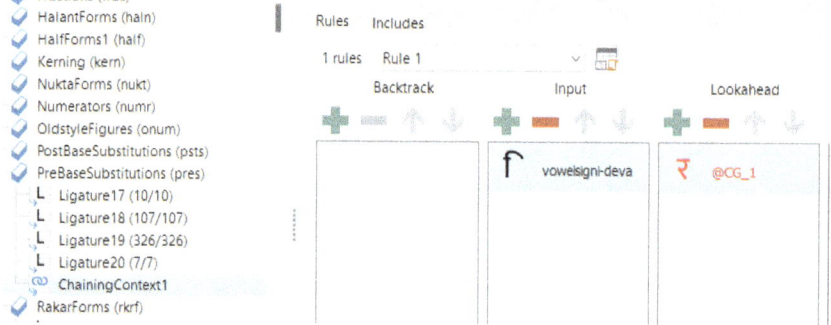

RakarForms (rkrf)

Feature = Ligature.
Ligature-replacing consonant+halant+repha combination glyphs with new drawn Ligature conjunct having back slash for repha. E.g. क्‌र→क्र where क्र is a new Ligature. (Not used in ट्‌र→ट्र where the repha becomes a caret i.e. circumflex, below some Consonants. For that the Feature = VattuVariants is used).

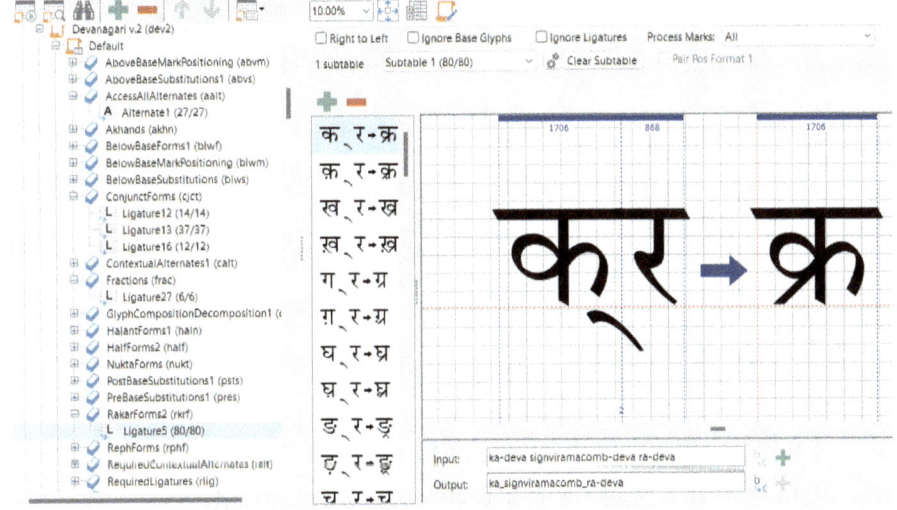

RephForms (rphf)

Feature = Ligature.
Ligature for replacing repha+halant glyphs with top curl glyph. Only this one Ligature र् →

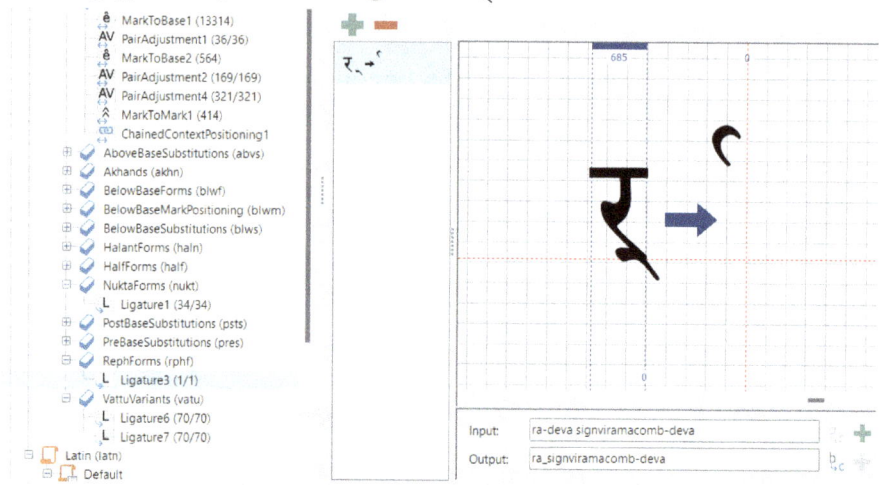

VattuVariants (vatu)

Ligature-replacing consonant+halant+repha combination glyphs with new drawn Ligature conjunct having caret below for repha. E.g. ट् र → ट्र where ट्र is a new Ligature.

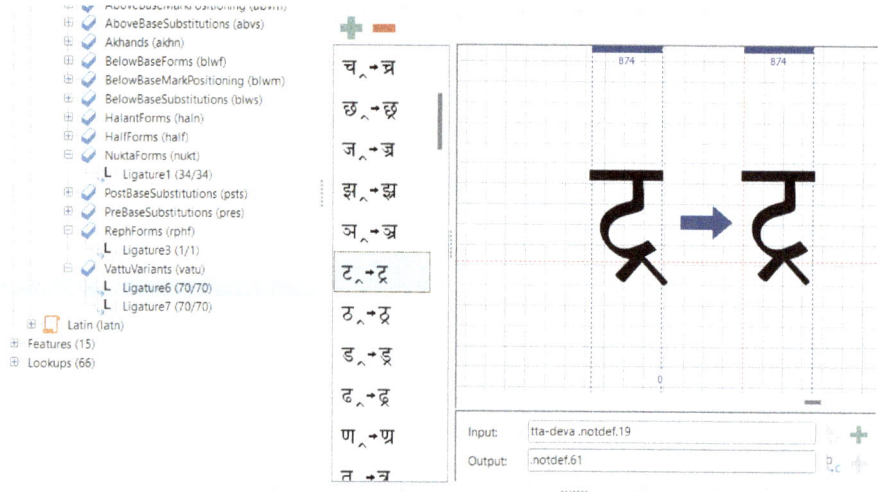

StylisticAlternates (salt)
Feature = SingleSubstitution.
Replacing a glyph with another glyph, for presentation.

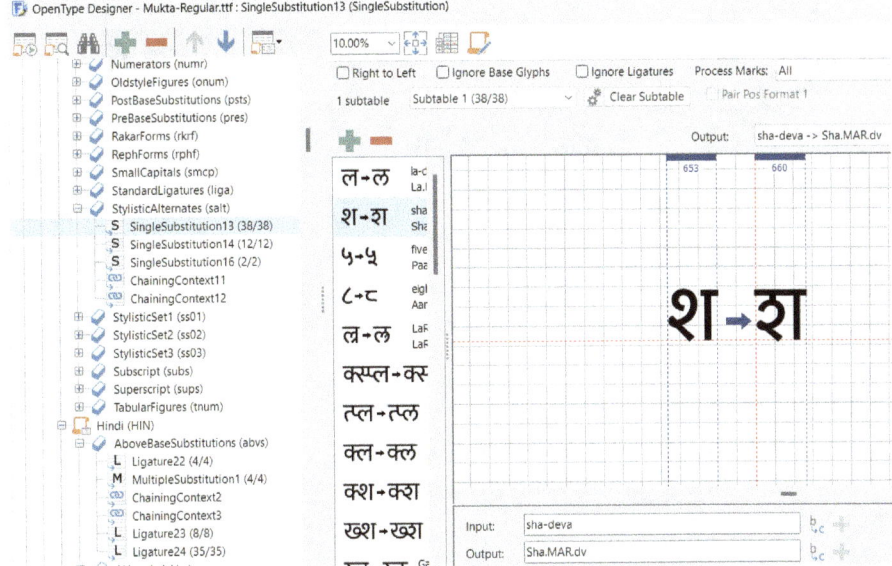

StylisticSet (ss)
Feature = SingleSubstitution.
Replacing a glyph with another glyph, for archaic use presentatlon.

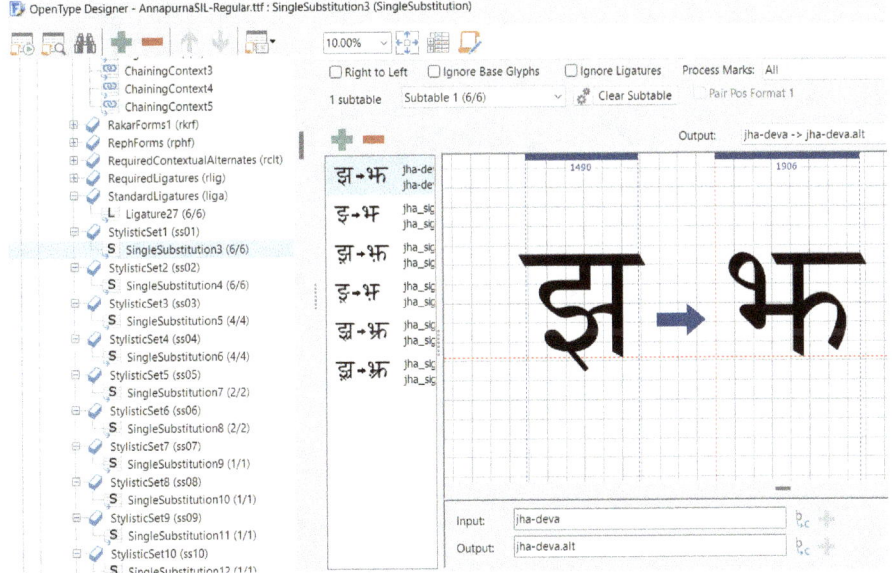

Kerning (kern)
Feature = PairAdjustment.
Adjusting gap between glyphs.

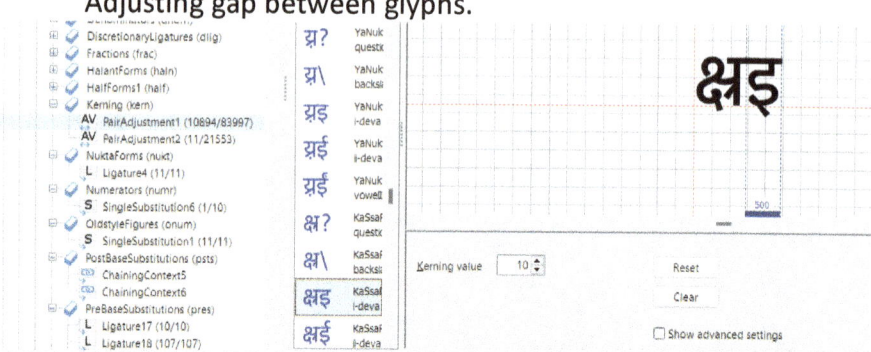

Distances (dist)
Feature = CursiveAttachment.
Adjusting gap between glyphs.

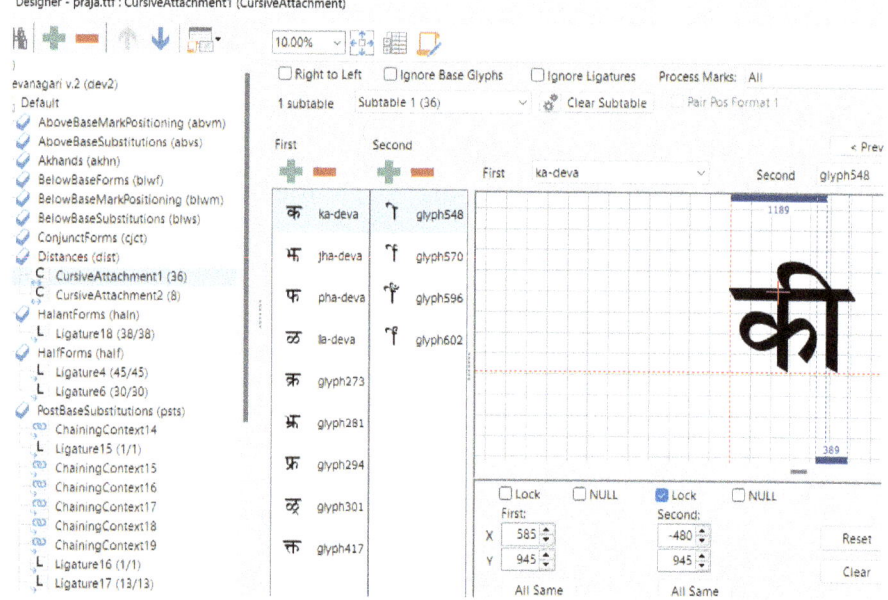

Devanagari Character Glyph Class Scheme

An important part of Devanagari Font creation is knowing the class of each glyph and character from Unicode Block. Then we can attach and position them correctly.

A proposed character class scheme for correct implementation of Sanskrit Typesetting is outlined here, so that
- Unicode Developers
- Script Developers
- Font Developers
- Open Type Design Shaping Engine Developers

can help users in writing "correct and beautiful Sanskrit" texts and books and documents as per the extant Ancient Sanskrit Literature, in the modern world.

The following is a proposed class scheme for the principal Devanagari Unicode Blocks used by any Sanskrit font.

NS = **Not in Sanskrit** usage/Dravidian etc.

IU = Indirect Use.

V = Vowel.

C = **Consonant** with inherent vowel.

M = **Matra** of Vowel Sign. Only one Matra out of the set can be attached to a Consonant or Conjunct.

N = **Nasalization** or Visarga Sign. Can attach to Vowel or Consonant or Conjunct, with or without Matra. Only one of these can attach simultaneously.

A = **Accent** or Stress Sign. Only one Accent out of the set can be attached to a Vowel or Consonant, with or without Matra.

S = **Sandhi** Symbol.

P = **Punctuation** Symbol.

OM = Sacred Symbol.

E = **Extended Nukta** Sign. Can attach to a Consonant with or without Matra.

H = Vowel Suppress **Halant** Sign. Can attach only to a Consonant.

O = **Numeral**. Ordinal.

IU = Insignificant Use Consonant.

In a Open type design software,
the Symbols are independent glyphs, while
the Signs are dependent glyphs.

Hence when we insert a Symbol in MS Word, it is directly typed. However when we insert a Sign in MS Word it is seen with a geometric shape dotted circle, to signify that some other glyph should precede it first, and it will attach to that glyph.

==Make new glyphs in Sanskrit 2023 for signs with dotted circle.==

Devanagari Block = Unicode U+0900 to 097F
128 characters with glyphs

0900	0901	0902	0903	0904	0905	0906	0907
ऀ	ँ	ं	ः	ऄ	अ	आ	इ
N	N	N	N	NS	V	V	V

0908	0909	090A	090B	090C	090D	090E	090F
ई	उ	ऊ	ऋ	ऌ	ऍ	ऎ	ए
V	V	V	V	V	NS	NS	V

0910	0911	0912	0913	0914	0915	0916	0917
ऐ	ऑ	ऒ	ओ	औ	क	ख	ग
V	NS	NS	V	V	C	C	C

0918	0919	091A	091B	091C	091D	091E	091F
घ	ङ	च	छ	ज	झ	ञ	ट
C	C	C	C	C	C	C	C

0920	0921	0922	0923	0924	0925	0926	0927
ठ	ड	ढ	ण	त	थ	द	ध
C	C	C	C	C	C	C	C

0928	0929	092A	092B	092C	092D	092E	092F
न	ऩ	प	फ	ब	भ	म	य
C	C	C	C	C	C	C	C

0930	0931	0932	0933	0934	0935	0936	0937
र	ऱ	ल	ळ	ऴ	व	श	ष
C	NS	C	C	NS	C	C	C

0938	0939	093A	093B	093C	093D	093E	093F
स	ह	ऺ	ऻ	़	ऽ	ा	ि
C	C	NS	NS	E	S	M	M

0940	0941	0942	0943	0944	0945	0946	0947
ी	ु	ू	ृ	ॄ	ॅ	ॆ	े
M	M	M	M	M	NS	NS	M

0948	0949	094A	094B	094C	094D	094E	094F
ै	ॉ	ॊ	ो	ौ	्	ॎ	ॏ
M	NS	NS	M	M	H	NS	NS

0950	0951	0952	0953	0954	0955	0956	0957
ॐ	॑	॒	॓	॔	ॕ	ॖ	ॗ
OM	A	A	NS	NS	NS	NS	NS

0958	0959	095A	095B	095C	095D	095E	095F
क़	ख़	ग़	ज़	ड़	ढ़	फ़	य़
IU	IU	IU	IU	IU	IU	IU	IU

0960	0961	0962	0963	0964	0965	0966	0967
ॠ	ॡ	ॢ	ॣ	।	॥	०	१
V	V	M	M	P	P	O	O

0968	0969	096A	096B	096C	096D	096E	096F
२	३	४	५	६	७	८	९
O	O	O	O	O	O	O	O

0970	0971	0972	0973	0974	0975	0976	0977
॰	ॱ	ॲ	ॳ	ॴ	ॵ	ॶ	ॷ
P	P	NS	NS	NS	NS	NS	NS

0978	0979	097A	097B	097C	097D	097E	097F
ॸ	ॹ	ॺ	ॻ	ॼ	ॽ	ॾ	ॿ
NS	NS	C	NS	NS	NS	NS	NS

Vedic Extensions Block = Unicode 1CD0 to 1CFF

48 characters with 43 glyphs and last 5 Unallocated.

Legend

AO = **Accent On Numeral** Sign. Usually attaches to Numerals.

VA = **Visarga Accent** Sign. Can attach only to Visarga.

GA = **Gomukha Anusvara** Symbol. Long Anusvara Symbol. Usually the Anusvara Sign is additionally attached to a Gomukha. Refer Combining Diacritical Marks Supplement Block.

GT = **Gomukha Tiryak** Sign. Can attach only to a Gomukha.

SA = Special Anusvara Symbol.

P = Punctuation Symbol.

A = **Accent** Sign. Stress Sign.

NS = **Not in Sanskrit** Language. Used in Dravidian, Bhojpuri etc.

1CD0	1CD1	1CD2	1CD3	1CD4	1CD5	1CD6	1CD7
ˆ	↑	−	″	−			
AO	AO	AO	P	A	A	A	A

1CD8	1CD9	1CDA	1CDB	1CDC	1CDD	1CDE	1CDF
−	^	‖	‖‖	ǀ	·	··	···
A	A	A	A	A	A	A	A

1CE0	1CE1	1CE2	1CE3	1CE4	1CE5	1CE6	1CE7
⌒	ʃ	−	⟩	⟨	⟨	⟩	ʂ
NS	P	VA	VA	VA	VA	VA	VA

1CE8	1CE9	1CEA	1CEB	1CEC	1CED	1CEE	1CEF
ៜ	꜠	꜡	Ꜣ	ꜣ	ˋ	ꜤE	ꜥE
VA	GA	GA	GA	GA	GT	SA	SA

1CF0	1CF1	1CF2	1CF3	1CF4	1CF5	1CF6	1CF7
ꜦE	ꜧE	Ꜩ	ꜩ	ꜪE	ꜫ	Ꜭ	ʃ
SA	SA	N	N	A	NS	NS	P

1CF8	1CF9	1CFA	1CFB	1CFC	1CFD	1CFE	1CFF
˚	˚˚	ꜭE					
A	A	GA					

Devanagari Extended Block = Unicode A8E0 to A8FF

32 characters with glyphs.

Legend
AV = Samaveda Accent Sign. AV signs are Accents attached above. To Vowels; and Consonants with Inherent vowel, with or without Matra. These are non-spacing signs.
IN = Independent Nasal Anusvara Symbol.
AH = Headstroke Accent Sign.
SS = Sacred Siddham Symbol.
P = Punctuation Symbol.
NS = **Not in Sanskrit** Language. Used in Dravidian, Bhojpuri etc.

A8E0	A8E1	A8E2	A8E3	A8E4	A8E5	A8E6	A8E7
०	१	२	३	४	५	६	७
AV	AV	AV	AV	AV	AV	AV	AV

A8E8	A8E9	A8EA	A8EB	A8EC	A8ED	A8EE	A8EF
८	९	अ	उ	क	न	प	र
AV	AV	AV	AV	AV	AV	AV	AV

AV signs are Accents attached above to
- Vowels and
- Consonants with Inherent vowel, with or without Matra.

A8F0	A8F1	A8F2	A8F3	A8F4	A8F5	A8F6	A8F7
वि	ऽ	ꣲ	ꣳ	ꣴ	ꣵ	ꣶ	ꣷ
AV	AV	IN	IN	IN	IN	IN	IN

A8F8	A8F9	A8FA	A8FB	A8FC	A8FD	A8FE	A8FF
꣸	꣹	꣺	ꣻ	꣼	ꣽ	ꣾ	ꣿ
P	P	P	AH	SS	NS	NS	NS

अ आ इ ई उ ऊ ऋ ॠ ऌ ॡ ए ऐ ओ औ अं अः ।
अ॒ अ॑ अँ अं अः Devanagari

अ॒ अ॒ अ॒ अ॒ अ॒ अँ अँ अ॒ अ॒ अ॒ अ॒ अ᳽ अ᳽ ऑ ऑ ऑ
Vedic Extensions

१ २ ३ ४ ५ ६ ७ ८ ९ ० अ उ क न प र वि ऽ
꣠ ꣡ ꣢ ꣣ ꣤ ꣥ ꣦ ꣧ ꣨ ꣩ ꣪ ꣫ ꣬ ꣭ ꣮ ꣯ ꣰ ꣱ अ̆
अ̆ Devanagari Extended

Font Programming - Correct placement of Accent, Matra, Bindu, Nukta using Anchors

Software/ platform	Apple mac	Microsoft Word	LibreOffice	Google Android
Shaping engine	Coretext ???	Uniscribe/Dwrite	harfbuzz	harfbuzz

Any Unicode character is a glyph (symbol).

To see its exact place in the Unicode character set, in hexadecimal.

The character code, ALT+X

For example, to insert the euro currency symbol €, press **20AC**, and then hold down the ALT key and press X.

Note
- pres, psts, mkmk, mark are standard OpenTypeDesign Features whereas
- blws, abvs, psts, abvm, blwm are specific to Indic Language design support only

Implementation in font design using high-logic font editor.
- Position anchors in the Glyphs window and not in OpenType designer. Fine tune the anchors if needed in the designer.
- Search for anchors using find in code editor in designer.
- Associated Anchors will have an arrow mark. Unassociated anchors will have no mark, as seen in Anchors window.
- Each base glyph has an anchor point that is defined with the

  left X and Y value and is indicated by the anchor icon: Modifying these values will change the location of the mark glyph.
- Each mark glyph also has an anchor point that is defined with the right X and Y value. Modifying these values will change the location where the mark glyph will be drawn in relation to the base glyph anchor.

In short:

- Modify left X,Y: Change position of all marks in relation to the base glyph
- Modify right X,Y: Change position of mark in relation to all base glyphs

Note:
- For vowels with inbuilt top matra ii ई, ai ऐ, o ओ, au औ we may use new glyph ligature substitution if needed.
- For r+u रु , r+uu रू , h+ri हृ , h+rri हॄ , h+li हॢ we use new glyph ligature substitution
- For r+ai रै we use kerning pair since the width of repha is very small.
- For r+i रि we use prebase ChainingContext SingleSubstitution.
- For iVowelsign+candrabindu िँ , iVowelsign+anusvara िं , iVowelsign+repha िर् , we use postbase ligature substitution with flags IgnoreBaseGlyphs, IgnoreLigatures.
- Anusavara Gomukha work using single substitution with new ligature glyph that has anusvaraOnGomukha. ७ ं

कि खि गि घि ङि चि छि जि झि ञि टि ठि डि ढि णि ति थि दि धि नि पि फि बि भि मि यि रि लि वि शि षि सि हि य
कि खि गि रि रि रि की खी गी री के खे गे कै खै गै रै कौ खौ गौ रौ कौ खौ गौ रौ टि टि रि
रि रि कि कि कि
कि कि कि (abvm)markTomark की कौ कौ की कौ कौ की कौ कौ के कै के कै कै कै
In mark-to-mark, the anchor is base in one and mark in another, however both glyphs are mark glyphs in glyph properties window.

Sample Typing using Sanskrit 2020 font

अ आ इ ई उ ऊ ऋ ॠ ऌ ए ऐ ओ औ
अं आं इं ईं उं ऊं ऋं ॠं ऌं एं ऐं ओं औं
अँ आँ इँ ईँ उँ ऊँ ऋँ ॠँ ऌँ एँ ऐँ ओँ औँ
अः आः इः ईः उः ऊः ऋः ॠः ऌः एः ऐः ओः औः
ईं ईं यँ ईं क्षँ ज्ञँ यऻ ० ं ० ं ० ं ० ं

क ख ग घ ङ च छ ज झ ञ ट ठ ड ढ ण त थ द ध न प फ ब भ म य र ल व श ष स ह
ळ य

हरिः हरः हरिः हरः हरीः हरिः हरिऺ ड्ड ट्ट ठ्ठ ड्ड ह्ह छ्छ

क् ख् ग् घ् ङ् च् छ् ज् झ् ञ् ट् ठ् ड् ढ् ण् त् थ् द् ध् न् प् फ् ब् भ् म् य् र् ल् व् श् ष् स् ह्
ळ् य्
कं खं गं घं ङं चं छं जं झं ञं टं ठं डं ढं णं तं थं दं धं नं पं फं बं भं मं यं रं लं वं शं षं सं हं
ळं यं
कँ खँ गँ घँ ङँ चँ छँ जँ झँ ञँ टँ ठँ डँ ढँ णँ तँ थँ दँ धँ नँ पँ फँ बँ भँ मँ यँ रँ लँ वँ शँ षँ सँ हँ
ळँ यँ
कः खः गः घः ङः चः छः जः झः ञः टः ठः डः ढः णः तः थः दः धः नः पः फः बः
भः मः यः रः लः वः शः षः सः हः ळः यः

कूः खूः गैः घैः ङोैः चौः छः जः झः ञः टः ठः डः ढः णः तः थः दः धः नः पः फः बः भः
मः यः रः लः वः शः षः सः हः ळः यः

का खा गा घा ङा चा छा जा झा ञा टा ठा डा ढा णा ता था दा धा ना पा फा बा भा मा या
रा ला वा शा षा सा हा ळा या

कि खि गि घि ङि चि छि जि झि ञि टि ठि डि ढि णि ति थि दि धि नि पि फि बि भि मि यि
रि लि वि शि षि सि हि ळि यि

की खी गी घी ङी ची छी जी झी ञी टी ठी डी ढी णी ती थी दी धी नी पी फी बी भी मी यी री ली वी शी षी सी ही ळी य़ी

कु खु गु घु ङु चु छु जु झु ञु टु ठु डु ढु णु तु थु दु धु नु पु फु बु भु मु यु रु लु वु शु षु सु हु ळु य़ु

कू खू गू घू ङू चू छू जू झू ञू टू ठू डू ढू णू तू थू दू धू नू पू फू बू भू मू यू रू लू वू शू षू सू हू ळू य़ू

कृ खृ गृ घृ ङृ चृ छृ जृ झृ ञृ टृ ठृ डृ ढृ णृ तृ थृ दृ धृ नृ पृ फृ बृ भृ मृ यृ ऋ लृ वृ शृ षृ सृ हृ ळृ य़ृ

कॄ खॄ गॄ घॄ ङॄ चॄ छॄ जॄ झॄ ञॄ टॄ ठॄ डॄ ढॄ णॄ तॄ थॄ दॄ धॄ नॄ पॄ फॄ बॄ भॄ मॄ यॄ ॠ लॄ वॄ शॄ षॄ सॄ हॄ ळॄ य़ॄ

कॢ खॢ गॢ घॢ ङॢ चॢ छॢ जॢ झॢ ञॢ टॢ ठॢ डॢ ढॢ णॢ तॢ थॢ दॢ धॢ नॢ पॢ फॢ बॢ भॢ मॢ यॢ ॡ लॢ वॢ शॢ षॢ सॢ हॢ ळॢ य़ॢ

के खे गे घे ङे चे छे जे झे ञे टे ठे डे ढे णे ते थे दे धे ने पे फे बे भे मे ये रे ले वे शे षे से हे ळे य़े

कै खै गै घै ङै चै छै जै झै ञै टै ठै डै ढै णै तै थै दै धै नै पै फै बै भै मै यै रै लै वै शै षै सै है ळै य़ै

को खो गो घो ङो चो छो जो झो ञो टो ठो डो ढो णो तो थो दो धो नो पो फो बो भो मो यो रो लो वो शो षो सो हो ळो य़ो

कौ खौ गौ घौ ङौ चौ छौ जौ झौ ञौ टौ ठौ डौ ढौ णौ तौ थौ दौ धौ नौ पौ फौ बौ भौ मौ यौ रौ लौ वौ शौ षौ सौ हौ ळौ य़ौ

कां खां गां घां ङां चां छां जां झां जां टां ठां डां ढां णां तां थां दां धां नां पां फां बां भां मां यां रां लां वां शां षां सां हां ळां य

कि खि गि घि ङि चि छि जि झि जि टि ठि डि ढि णि ति थि दि धि नि पि फि बि भि मि यि रि लि वि शि षि सि हि ळि य

कि खि गि घि ङि चि छि जि झि जि टि ठि डि ढि णि ति थि दि धि नि पि फि बि भि मि यि रि लि वि शि षि सि हि ळि य

की खी गी घी ङी ची छी जी झी जी टी ठी डी ढी णी ती थी दी धी नी पी फी बी भी मी यी री ली वी शी षी सी ही ळी य

के खे गे घे ङे चे छे जे झे जे टे ठे डे ढे णे ते थे दे धे ने पे फे बे भे मे ये रे ले वे शे षे से हे ळे य
के खे गे घे ङे चे छे जे झे जे टे ठे डे ढे णे ते थे दे धे ने पे फे बे भे मे ये रे ले वे शे षे से हे ळे य

कों खों गों घों ङों चों छों जों झों जों टों ठों डों ढों णों तों थों दों धों नों पों फों बों भों मों यों रों लों वों शों षों सों हों ळों य
कों खों गों घों ङों चों छों जों झों जों टों ठों डों ढों णों तों थों दों धों नों पों फों बों भों मों यों रों लों वों शों षों सों हों ळों य

कां खां गां घां ङां चां छां जां झां जां टां ठां डां ढां णां तां थां दां धां नां पां फां बां भां मां यां रां लां वां शां षां सां हां ळां य
कीं खीं गीं घीं ङीं चीं छीं जीं झीं जीं टीं ठीं डीं ढीं णीं तीं थीं दीं धीं नीं पीं फीं बीं भीं मीं यीं रीं लीं वीं शीं षीं सीं हीं ळीं य

कें खें गें घें ङें चें छें जें झें जें टें ठें डें ढें णें तें थें दें धें नें पें फें बें भें में यें रें लें वें शें षें सें हें ळें य

99

कें खें गें घें ङें चें छें जें झें ञें टें ठें डें ढें णें तें थें दें धें नें पें फें बें भें में यें रें लें वें शें षें सें हें ळें ब

कों खों गों घों ङों चों छों जों झों ञों टों ठों डों ढों णों तों थों दों धों नों पों फों बों भों मों यों रों लों वों शों षों सों हों ळों ब

कौं खौं गौं घौं ङौं चौं छौं जौं झौं ञौं टौं ठौं डौं ढौं णौं तौं थौं दौं धौं नौं पौं फौं बौं भौं मौं यौं रौं लौं वौं शौं षौं सौं हौं ळौं ब

क ख ग घ ङ च छ ज झ ञ ट ठ ड ढ ण त थ द ध न प फ ब भ म य र ल व श ष स ह ळ ब

क ख ग घ ङ च छ ज झ ञ ट ठ ड ढ ण त थ द ध न प फ ब भ म य र ल व श ष स ह ळ ब

क ख ग घ ङ च छ ज झ ञ ट ठ ड ढ ण त थ द ध न प फ ब भ म य र ल व श ष स ह ळ ब

का खा गा रा कि खि गि रि की खी गी री के खे गे रे कै खै गै रै को खो गो रो कौ खौ गौ रौ

का खा गा रा कि खि गि रि की खी गी री के खे गे रे कै खै गै रै को खो गो रो कौ खौ गौ रौ

कां खां गां रां किं खिं गिं रिं कीं खीं गीं रीं कें खें गें रें कैं खैं गैं रैं कों खों गों रों कौं खौं गौं रौं

कां खां गां रां किं खिं गिं रिं कीं खीं गीं रीं कें खें गें रें कैं खैं गैं रैं कों खों गों रों कौं खौं गौं रौं

टें टौं टिं टीं टें टैं टों टौं कैं कों किं कीं कें कैं कों कौं सौं

कें कों खों गों रों किं खिं गिं रिं कीं खीं गीं रीं कें खें गें रें कैं खैं गैं रैं कों खों गों रों कौं खौं गौं रौं

कें कों खों गों रों किं खिं गिं रिं कीं खीं गीं रीं कें खें गें रें कैं खैं गैं रैं कों खों गों रों कौं खौं गौं रौं

कें कों खों गों रों किं खिं गिं रिं कीं खीं गीं रीं कें खें गें रें कैं खैं गैं रैं कों खों गों रों कौं खौं गौं रौं

कें कों खों गों रों किं खिं गिं रिं कीं खीं गीं रीं कें खें गें रें कैं खैं गैं रैं कों खों गों रों कौं खौं गौं रौं

क ख ग् घ ङ कु कू कृ कॄ कॢ कु कू कृ कॄ कॢ
कु कू कृ कॄ कॢ कु कू कृ कॄ कॢ कु कू कृ कॄ कॢ

क् ख् ग् घ् ङ् कु कू कृ कॄ कॢ

कु कू कृ कॄ कॢ कु कू कृ कॄ कॢ कु कू कृ कॄ कॢ

कॆ खॆ ङॆ ऒ ऱ ऴ

क ख ग् घ ङ कु कू कृ कॄ कॢ कु कू कृ कॄ कॢ
कु कू कृ कॄ कॢ कु कू कृ कॄ कॢ

खं खां कं कां कः कं कँ कँ कि कें कैं

खं खां कं कां कंः

खं खां कं कां कः कं कँ कँ कि कें कैं कीं कें कैं कौं कौं

क का कः कं कँ कँ कि की के कै को कौ कि की कें कैं कौं कौं

The glyphs 1CE2   1CE3   1CE4   1CE5   1CE6   1CE7   1CE8   are for visarga only. Check their proper attachment. They should not be attachable to other consonants.

कः कः कः कः कः कः कः

कीखीं कें कें कें कें कों कों कँ कँ कँ कँ कँ कँ कँ कँ
कः कुः कूः कृः कः कः कः कꣳ कꣳ कꣳ कꣳ

काꣳ कीꣳ कूꣳ कोꣳ कृः कः क्ः कꣳ क कुः कृ कृः क्ः कृ कि
की कें कें कौं कों कि की कें कें कौं कों कि की कें कें कौं कों

कि की कें कें कौं कों कि की कें कें कौं कों कि की कें कें
कौं कों कं कं कं कं कं कं

कँ कꣳ कꣳ कꣳ कꣳ कꣳ ꣡ ꣢ कँ कर ꣢ ꣣ ऍ कैं
खीं खें खें खों खों खं खं
कं खं गं घं ङं चं छं जं झं ञं टं ठं डं ढं णं तं थं दं धं नं पं फं
बं भं मं यं रं लं वं शं षं सं हं
रं रां रिं रीं रुं रूं ऋं ऌं ॠं ॡं रें रैं रों रौं
खं खं खं खं खं खं खं खं खं खं खं खं खं खं खं खं
खं खं

कं खं गं घं ङं चं छं जं झं ञं टं ठं डं ढं णं तं थं दं धं नं पं फं
बं भं मं यं रं लं वं शं षं सं हं

कें खें गें घें ङें चें छें जें झें ञें टें ठें डें ढें णें तें थें दें धें नें पें फें
बें भें में यें रें लें वें शें षें सें हें

कँ खँ गँ घँ ङँ चँ छँ जँ झँ ञँ टँ ठँ डँ ढँ णँ तँ थँ दँ धँ नँ पँ
फँ बँ भँ मँ यँ रँ लँ वँ शँ षँ सँ हँ

कैं खैं गैं घैं ङैं चैं छैं जैं झैं ञैं टैं ठैं डैं ढैं णैं तैं थैं दैं धैं नैं पैं फैं
बैं भैं मैं यैं रैं लैं वैं शैं षैं सैं हैं
कैँ खैँ गैँ घैँ ङैँ चैँ छैँ जैँ झैँ ञैँ टैँ ठैँ डैँ ढैँ णैँ तैँ थैँ दैँ धैँ नैँ पैँ
फैँ बैँ भैँ मैँ यैँ रैँ लैँ वैँ शैँ षैँ सैँ हैँ

कैं खैं गैं घैं ङैं चैं छैं जैं झैं ञैं टैं ठैं डैं ढैं णैं तैं थैं दैं
धैं नैं पैं फैं बैं भैं मैं यैं रैं लैं वैं शैं षैं सैं हैं

कों खों गों घों ङों चों छों जों झों ञों टों ठों डों ढों णों तों थों
दों धों नों पों फों बों भों मों यों रों लों वों शों षों सों हों

कोँ खोँ गोँ घोँ ङोँ चोँ छोँ जोँ झोँ ञोँ टोँ ठोँ डोँ ढोँ णोँ तोँ थोँ
दोँ धोँ नोँ पोँ फोँ बोँ भोँ मोँ योँ रोँ लोँ वोँ शोँ षोँ सोँ होँ

कौं खौं गौं घौं ङौं चौं छौं जौं झौं ञौं टौं ठौं डौं ढौं णौं तौं थौं
दौं धौं नौं पौं फौं बौं भौं मौं यौं रौं लौं वौं शौं षौं सौं हौं
कौं खौं गौं घौं ङौं चौं छौं जौं झौं ञौं टौं ठौं डौं ढौं णौं तौं थौं
दौं धौं नौं पौं फौं बौं भौं मौं यौं रौं लौं वौं शौं षौं सौं हौं
कौं खौं गौं घौं ङौं चौं छौं जौं झौं ञौं टौं ठौं डौं ढौं णौं तौं
थौं दौं धौं नौं पौं फौं बौं भौं मौं यौं रौं लौं वौं शौं षौं सौं हौं
कौं खौं गौं घौं ङौं <mark>चौं</mark> छौं जौं झौं ञौं टौं ठौं डौं ढौं णौं तौं थौं
दौं धौं नौं पौं फौं बौं भौं मौं यौं रौं लौं वौं शौं षौं सौं हौं

कीं खीं गीं घीं ङीं चीं छीं जीं झीं ञीं टीं ठीं डीं ढीं णीं तीं थीं
दीं धीं नीं पीं फीं बीं भीं मीं यीं रीं लीं वीं शीं षीं सीं हीं

कीं खीं गीं घीं ङीं चीं छीं जीं झीं ञीं टीं ठीं डीं ढीं णीं तीं थीं
दीं धीं नीं पीं फीं बीं भीं मीं यीं रीं लीं वीं शीं षीं सीं हीं

कीं खीं गीं घीं ङीं चीं छीं जीं झीं ञीं टीं ठीं डीं ढीं णीं तीं थीं
दीं धीं नीं पीं फीं बीं भीं मीं यीं रीं लीं वीं शीं षीं सीं हीं

कं खं गं घं ङं चं छं जं झं ञं टं ठं डं ढं णं तं थं दं धं नं पं फं
बं भं मं यं रं लं वं शं षं सं हं
कं खं गं घं ङं चं छं जं झं ञं टं ठं डं ढं णं तं थं दं धं नं पं फं
बं भं मं यं रं लं वं शं षं सं हं

कँ खँ गँ घँ ङँ चँ छँ जँ झँ ञँ टँ ठँ डँ ढँ णँ तँ थँ दँ धँ नँ पँ फँ
बँ भँ मँ यँ रँ लँ वँ शँ षँ सँ हँ
कँ खँ गँ घँ ङँ चँ छँ जँ झँ ञँ टँ ठँ डँ ढँ णँ तँ थँ दँ धँ नँ पँ फँ
बँ भँ मँ यँ रँ लँ वँ शँ षँ सँ हँ

कँ खँ गँ घँ ङँ चँ छँ जँ झँ ञँ टँ ठँ डँ ढँ णँ तँ थँ दँ धँ नँ पँ
फँ बँ भँ मँ यँ रँ लँ वँ शँ षँ सँ हँ

कँ खँ गँ घँ ङँ चँ छँ जँ झँ ञँ टँ ठँ डँ ढँ णँ तँ थँ दँ धँ
नँ पँ फँ बँ भँ मँ यँ रँ लँ वँ शँ षँ सँ हँ

(double and triple svarita occupy space above turban of the following varna also and may obstruct their matra.) Use ligature substitution.

कं खं गं घं ङं चं छं जं झं ञं टं ठं डं ढं णं तं थं दं धं नं पं फं
बं भं मं यं रं लं वं शं षं सं हं

कं खं गं घं ङं चं छं जं झं ञं टं ठं डं ढं णं तं थं दं धं नं पं फं
बं भं मं यं रं लं वं शं षं सं हं

कँ खँ गँ घँ ङँ चँ छँ जँ झँ ञँ टँ ठँ डँ ढँ णँ तँ थँ दँ धँ नँ पँ
फँ बँ भँ मँ यँ रँ लँ वँ शँ षँ सँ हँ

कॅ खॅ गॅ घॅ ङॅ चॅ छॅ जॅ झॅ ञॅ टॅ ठॅ डॅ ढॅ णॅ तॅ थॅ दॅ धॅ नॅ पॅ फॅ
बॅ भॅ मॅ यॅ रॅ लॅ वॅ शॅ षॅ सॅ हॅ

कॆ खॆ गॆ घॆ ङॆ चॆ छॆ जॆ झॆ ञॆ टॆ ठॆ डॆ ढॆ णॆ तॆ थॆ दॆ धॆ नॆ पॆ फॆ
बॆ भॆ मॆ यॆ रॆ लॆ वॆ शॆ षॆ सॆ हॆ

कॖ खॖ गॖ घॖ ङॖ चॖ छॖ जॖ झॖ ञॖ टॖ ठॖ डॖ ढॖ णॖ तॖ थॖ दॖ
धॖ नॖ पॖ फॖ बॖ भॖ मॖ यॖ रॖ लॖ वॖ शॖ षॖ सॖ हॖ

कॗ खॗ गॗ घॗ ङॗ चॗ छॗ जॗ झॗ ञॗ टॗ ठॗ डॗ ढॗ णॗ तॗ थॗ दॗ धॗ नॗ
पॗ फॗ बॗ भॗ मॗ यॗ रॗ लॗ वॗ शॗ षॗ सॗ हॗ

कँॗ खँॗ गँॗ घँॗ ङँॗ चँॗ छँॗ जँॗ झँॗ ञँॗ टँॗ ठँॗ डँॗ ढँॗ णँॗ तँॗ थँॗ दँॗ
धँॗ नँॗ पँॗ फँॗ बँॗ भँॗ मँॗ

यॗ रॗ   here left and right kern spacing is to be corrected in the glyph.
लँॗ वँॗ

Check the right side bearing for these glyphs.

कँ खँ गँ घँ ङँ चँ छँ जँ झँ ञँ टँ ठँ डँ ढँ णँ तँ
थँ दँ धँ नँ पँ फँ बँ भँ मँ यँ रँ लँ वँ शँ षँ सँ हँ
ऐं ईं औं ओं ऐं ईं औं ओं ऐं ईं औं ओं ऐं ईं औं ओं

Check and correct

औं ओं ऐं ईं औं ओं कां नां कं
ऐं ईं औं ओं ऐं ईं औं ओं ऐं ऐं ईं
ईं औं औं ओं

Positioning 4 or more glyphs

Positioning 4 glyphs is a challenge. ह ि ः ॑
(base+matra+visarga+svarita $0951).

The svarita $0951 always intersects. We need to position it a bit to the right so that it does not intersect the top matra. It should get positioned similar to anudatta $0952. E.g.

हरिः हरीः हरेः हरैः हरोः हरौः

(note: svarita is called udatta in unicode).

We achieved it using a composite ligature substitution!

हरिः हरीः हरेः हरैः हरोः हरौः

Use Composite glyph rather than combining

If a composite glyph is available, use it instead of combining two or more independent glyphs from the character sets.

Challenges of incorrect ligatures

Svarita Accent Placement with Top Repha

- र्धं र्कं र्डं र्खं र्कं
- र्धं र्कं र्डं र्खं र्कं र्गं र्घं र्लं पुष्टिवर्धनम्
- क का कि की कु कू कृ कॣ के कै को कौ कं कः ।
- कं कां किं कीं कुं कूं कृं कॣं कें कैं कों कौं कंं कःं । size of bottom vocalic li matra is huge.
- कं कां किं कीं कुं कूं कृं कॣं कें कैं कों कौं कंं कःं ।
- क का कि की कु कू कृ कॣ के कै को कौ कं कः ।

Svarita Accent with Anusvara

- अं आं इं ईं उं ऊं ऋं ॠं ऌं एं ऐं ओं औं
- अं आं इं (ईं) उं ऊं ऋं ॠं ऌं एं ऐं ओं औं
- अं आं इं (ईं) उं ऊं ऋं ॠं ऌं एं ऐं ओं औं

कं कं किं किं कीं कैं कैं कीं   कं कं किं कीं कैं कैं

Anudatta Accent with Visarga

अः अँ आः इ ई उ ऊ ऋ ॠ ऌ ए ऐ ओ औ अं अः अः

अ आ इ ई उ ऊ ऋ ॠ ऌ ए ऐ ओ औ अं अः anudatta here got shifted correctly due to markTomark positioning!

अः आः इः ईः उः ऊः ऋः ॠः ऌः एः ऐः ओः औः अं

क॒ कृ॒ को॒ की॒ क॒ः ख॒ः

Anudatta Accent with Bottom Matra/Conjunct

Classic example of incorrect Anudatta Accent placement with Bottom matra in common fonts.

Sanskrit 2003 युप॒ कृ॒ and Sanskrit 2020 ok युप॒ कृ॒

Arial Unicode युप॒ कृ॒

Sakal Bharati युप॒ कृ॒

CDAC Dhruv युप॒ कृ॒

Annapurna SIL युप॒ कृ॒

Adishila युप॒ कृ॒ and Siddhanta ok युप॒ कृ॒

Dirgha Svarita Accent Placement with TOP Matra

Classic example of incorrect Dirgha Svarita Accent placement. NA = Not Available. NAU= Not Available in correct unicode space

Sanskrit 2003 कै NAU

Arial Unicode कै NA

CDAC Dhruv कै NA

Annapurna SIL कै NA

Adishila touches the matra कै̎ किं̎ की̎

Siddhanta is fine कै̎ किं̎ की̎

Added unicode block Vedic Extensions. Dirgha svarita Glyph 1CDA
Copied glyph from Private Use Area glyph E008 to 1CDA.
Note – in word 2019 it shows as Buginese Unicode Block. Perhaps Vedic Extensions was not implemented completely in MS Word 2019 version.

Sanskrit 2020 कै̎ किं̎ की̎

क का कि की कु कू कृ कॢ के कै को कौ कं कः

devanagaristresssignudattacomb

क॑ का॑ कि॑ की॑ कु॑ कू॑ कृ॑ कॢ॑ के॑ कै॑ को॑ कौ॑ कं॑ कः॑

vedictonedoublesvaritacomb

क̎ का̎ कि̎ की̎ कु̎ कू̎ कृ̎ कॢ̎ के̎ कै̎ को̎ कौ̎ कं̎ कः̎
क̎ का̎ कि̎ की̎ कु̎ कू̎ कृ̎ कॢ̎ के̎ कै̎ को̎ कौ̎ कं̎ कः̎
क̎ का̎ कि̎ की̎ कु̎ कू̎ कृ̎ कॢ̎ के̎ कै̎ को̎ कौ̎ कं̎ कः̎

Samaveda Accents 'Add Space Before/After Paragraph'

For visibility of the typed tones in Samaveda, we need to use correct paragraph spacing.

अ आ इ ई ऐ औ अ आ इ ई ऐ औ अ आ इ ई ऐ औ ई ऐ औ Check and correct

अग्नआ याहि वीतये गृणानोहव्यदातये ।
नि होता सत्सि बर्हिषि ॥ १ ॥
ओग्ना इ । आयाही३ वीइयार॰इ ।
आनोविश्वासुहव्यमिन्द्र॰समत्सुभूषत ।

We have positioned accents above WinAscent, or below WinDescent, for proper size readability. Hence in a text editor like MS Word, it is needed to use 'Add Space Before Paragraph' or 'Add Space After Paragraph' for these to render correctly.

Changes needed in the shaping engine

Gomukha Anusvara U+1CE9

Changes needed in the shaping engine in Open Type design, somewhere in the back-end of code or the implementation in MS Word editor. Gomukha Anusvaras are blocked from combining with Anusvara and Candrabindu.

ਁ ਁ should be actually ਁ ਁ ਁ ਁ ਁ ਁ ਁ ਁ ਁ

Work around to implement them in a Devanagari font for now. Simply insert new characters in Private Use Area, and draw the correct ligatures. Then we can use Insert-Symbol in a Word Editor to type these.

Heavy yya U+097A

य़ꣳ य़ा य़ꣳय़ य़ा य़ꣳ य़

glyph U+097A, how to attach to Vowel sign?
Always shows vowel sign with dotted circle. Perhaps hardcoded in shaping engine back-end.

य़ य़ा य़ी य़ू workaround.

Ardhavisarga U+1CF2

This symbol is not available in Sanskrit2003 font, and is available in updated Sanskrit 2020 font.
- Added ardhavisarga glyph 1CF2 in unicode block Vedic Extensions.
- Copied visarga 0903 to ardhavisarga glyph 1CF2.
- Copied candrabindu 0901 into 1CF2 and modified it to ardhavisarga.
- कᳲ अᳲ अः कः

- In glyph 1CF2 Anchor_4 already copied. We simply add code for anudatta. belowbasemarkpositioning-marktobase
- However it does not attach to Vowels or Consonants. Perhaps hardcoded. Work around.

Numeral १ and ३ Accents

१͘͜ ३͘͜ both accents needed simultaneously for these two numerals.

१̖ ३̖ Work around by new ligatures in Private Use Area.

Numeral २ Tones U+1CD0

२̂ २̑ २̄ these tones are only for the numeral २. Not to be used for any other Letter or Vowel or Consonant.

https://www.unicode.org/Public/13.0.0/ucd/IndicSyllabicCategory.txt
https://www.unicode.org/L2/L2021/21006-gomukha.pdf
https://docs.microsoft.com/en-us/typography/script-development/use
https://docs.microsoft.com/en-us/typography/script-development/devanagari

सु सा स्य सा सुसं, ӧ ȯ ӧ ȯ ȯ, १̖ ३̖, २̂ २̑ २̄

Accents for Candrabindu Virama U+A8F3

To implement anudatta and svarita for ꣳ Workaround by making new ligatures in Private Use Area.

ꣳ ꣳ॒ ꣳ॑ ꣳ᳚

ꣳ॒ ꣳ॒ ꣳ॑ ꣳ᳚

ॐ ꣽ

Nasalized semivowel

Maha Mrityunjaye Mantra Usually written as

त्र्यम्बकं यजामहे सुगन्धि पुष्टिवर्धनम् ।
उर्वारुकमिव बन्धनान् मृत्योर् मुक्षीय माऽमृतात् ॥

For teaching Sanskrit Grammar and pronunciation we will use Nasalized semivowel.

त्र्यम्बकयँ यजामहे सुगन्धि पुष्टिवर्धनम् ।
उर्वारुकमिव बन्धनान् मृत्योर् मुक्षीय माऽमृतात् ॥

Indic Shaping and Spell Check Requirements

Listing our understanding regarding Indic Shaping Requirements to prevent invalid Sanskrit word formation. Our Proposals regarding Sanskrit spell check or correct shaping engine coding. These are listed after a careful study of Sanskrit Literature, including Classical and Vedic, Rigveda, Samaveda, Shukla Yajurveda, Krishna Yajurveda, Atharvaveda. This section has been given because the harfbuzz shaping engine allows any combination of letters. That is a serious error in implementation. It must be avoided.

https://typedrawers.com/discussion/3870/attaching-a-devanagari-vedic-extensions-base-glyph-with-a-mark

Consider the Devanagari Unicode Block U+0900 to 097F = 128 glyphs.

From a purely Sanskrit Language point-of-view (wherein glyphs from Awadhi, Dravidian, etc. are not accounted for).

The characters herein are classified as:

- Base Glyph Vowel = U+0905 to 090C, 090F, 0910, 0913, 0914, 0960, 0961= 14 glyphs = V
- Base Glyph Consonant = U+0915 to 0928, 092A to 0930, 0932, 0933, 0935 to 0939, 097A = 35 glyphs = C
- Mark Glyph Matra Vowel Sign = U+093E to 0944, 0947, 0948, 094B, 094C, 0962, 0963 = 13 glyphs = M
- Mark Glyph Nasalization and Aspirate Signs = U+0900, 0901, 0902, 0903 = 4 glyphs = N
- Mark Glyph Accent Stress Sign = U+0951, 0952 = 2 glyphs = A

- Numerals = U+0966 to 0970 = 10 glyphs = D
- Punctuation Sign = U+0964, 0965 = 2 glyphs = P
- Sandhi Sign = U+093D = 1 glyph = S
- Halant Virama Sign = U+094D = 1 glyph = H

For the purposes of this discussion we have given arbitrary abbreviations:

V = Base Glyph Vowel

C = Base Glyph Consonant

M = Mark Glyph Matra Vowel Sign

N = Mark Glyph Nasalization and Aspirate Sign

A = Mark Glyph Accent Stress Sign

Indic Shaping properties must account for the following to create VALID SANSKRIT TEXT:

1. Base Glyph Vowel = **V should not attach** to Mark Glyph Matra Vowel Sign = **M**.
"**VM**" **is an invalid combination.** Indic shaping must prevent this.

e.g. U+0905+0940 is invalid. ऑी INVALID SANSKRIT.

2. Base Glyph Vowel = **V can attach** to **only one glyph** from the - Mark Glyph Nasalization and Aspirate Signs = **N**
 "**VNN**" **is an invalid combination.** Here the last typed glyph should erase any previous **N**.
e.g. U+0905+0901+0903 is invalid. 0905+0901+0901 is invalid.
अं: INVALID SANSKRIT.

3. Base Glyph Vowel = **V can attach** to **only one glyph** from the - Mark Glyph Accent Stress Sign = **A**
 "**VAA**" **is an invalid combination.** Here the last typed glyph should erase any previous **A**.
e.g. U+0905+0951+0952 is invalid. 0905+0951+0951 is invalid.
 INVALID SANSKRIT.

4. Base Glyph Vowel = **V can attach** to **only two glyphs** from glyph sets (**N, A**) with the provision that the two glyphs are from distinct glyph sets.
"VNA", "VAN" are valid combinations.
E.g. **U+0905+0901+0952 is valid.**

 VALID.

"VNAN", "VANA" are invalid. Here the last typed glyph should erase any previous **N, A if duplicate**.

 INVALID SANSKRIT.

 INVALID SANSKRIT.

5a. Ligatures consisting of Punctuation Sign **P** must be **prevented** in Indic shaping.
E.g. **U+0964+0901 is invalid. U+0965+0903 is invalid.**

🕆 INVALID SANSKRIT.

‖ः INVALID SANSKRIT. (correctly implemented in harfbuzz!)

5a. Ligatures consisting of Sandhi Sign **S** must be **prevented** in Indic shaping.
E.g. **U+093D+0902 is invalid. U+093D+0903 is invalid.**

ऽं INVALID SANSKRIT. (correctly implemented in harfbuzz!)

ऽः INVALID SANSKRIT.

ऽॄ INVALID SANSKRIT.

6. Ligatures consisting **only** of Numerals १ or ३ along with **both** the Accent signs **A** simultaneously are permitted. A single accent sign with these numerals is INVALID.

U+0967 + 0951 + 0952 (all three together) is valid. १̱̍ VALID.

U+0969 + 0951 + 0952 (all three together) is valid. ३̱̍ VALID.

U+0967 + 0951 is invalid. १̍ INVALID SANSKRIT.

U+0967 + 0952 is invalid. १̱ INVALID SANSKRIT.

U+0969 + 0951 is invalid. ३̍ INVALID SANSKRIT.

U+0969 + 0952 is invalid. ३̱ INVALID SANSKRIT.

7. Base Glyph Consonant = **C can attach** to **only one** Mark Glyph Matra Vowel Sign = **M**.
"CM" is a valid combination.
"CMM" is invalid. Indic shaping must prevent this by keeping only the last typed **M**.
E.g. **U+0915+093E+0940 is invalid.**

क␣ी INVALID SANSKRIT.

कू INVALID SANSKRIT.

8. Base Glyph Consonant = **C can attach** to **only three total glyphs** from glyph sets (**M, N, A**) with the provision that the three glyphs are from distinct glyph sets, and **CM** cluster precedes the others.
"CMNA", "CMAN", "CNA", "CAN" are valid combinations.
"CMNAN", "CMANA" are invalid. Here the last typed glyph should erase any previous **N, A if duplicate**.
E.g. **U+0915+093E+0902+0940+903 is invalid.**

कां: INVALID SANSKRIT.

9. With the use of Halant Virama Sign **H,** indic shaping must **select the appropriate consonant ligatures** if present in the font.

10. For **invalid** combinations, the dotted circle glyph 25CC **must show** if implemented in font. Or, such an invalid combination must not be typable at all!
e.g.

1. अ◌ी

2. अं◌ः

3. अ◌্

4. अं◌ः

5a. I◌ँ II◌ः   5b. ऽ◌ं ऽ◌ी

6. १◌ं ३◌্

7. का◌ी

8. का◌ः◌ं

120

Shaping Technical Terms in Unicode

Mark having Indic Shaping class = **None**
Devanagari Block **Independent Mark**
- Om = Sacred symbol

Diacritics having Indic Shaping class = **Bindu**
Devanagari Block **Dependent NonSpacing Mark**
- CANDRABINDU, ANUSVARA = nazalization mark

Diacritic having Indic Shaping class = **Visarga**
Devanagari Block **Dependent Spacing Mark**
- VISARGA = air exhalation mark, subclass = Right Position

Diacritics having Indic Shaping class = **Cantillation**
Devanagari Block **Dependent NonSpacing Mark**
- Svarita = high pitch accent, subclass = Top Position
- Anudatta = low pitch accent, subclass = Bottom Position

Diacritic having Indic Shaping class = **Nukta**
Devanagari Block **Dependent NonSpacing Mark**
- NUKTA = tongue placement mark, subclass = Bottom Position

Diacritic having Indic Shaping class = **Virama**
Devanagari Block **Dependent NonSpacing Mark**
- HALANT = consonant vowel removal, subclass = Bottom Position

Letter having Indic Shaping class = **Avagraha**
Devanagari Block **Independent Letter**
- AVAGRAHA = indicates a dropped अ vowel

Punctuations having Indic Shaping class = **None**
Devanagari Block **Independent Punctuation**
- Danda = indicates a stop or pause in a verse
- Double Danda = indicates a full stop.
- Abbreviation Ring = indicates an abbreviated word.

Letters having Indic Shaping class = **Consonant**
Devanagari Block **Independent Letter**
- Consonant क ख ग घ ङ च छ ज झ ञ ट ठ ड ढ ण त थ द ध न प फ ब भ म य र ल व श ष स ह ळ य

Letters having Indic Shaping class = **Vowel**
Devanagari Block **Independent Letter**
- Vowels अ आ इ ई उ ऊ ऋ ॠ ऌ ॡ ए ऐ ओ औ

Marks having Indic Shaping class = **Vowel Matra**
Devanagari Block **Dependent Mark**
- Matras ा ि ी ु ू ृ ॄ ॢ ॣ े ै ो ौ

Vowel Matra subclass = **Matra Position**
- **Spacing** Matra Position Left = Prebase ि
- **Spacing** Matra Position Right = Postbase ा ी ो ौ
- **NonSpacing** Matra Position Top = Abovebase े ै
- **NonSpacing** Matra Bottom = Belowbase ु ू ृ ॄ ॢ ॣ

Numbers having Indic Shaping class = **Number**
Devanagari Block **Independent Number**
- Numbers १ २ ३ ४ ५ ६ ७ ८ ९ ०

Note:
Numbers १ २ ३ should have a special shaping class. This is so that the Vedic Tones U+1CD0, 1CD1, 1CD2 can get attached above to these numerals alone, and not to any other Letter, Vowel or Consonant.

Numbers १ ३ should have a special shaping class. This is so that the Vedic Accents Svarita U+0951, Anudatta U+0952, can **both** get attached **simultaneously** to these numerals alone. For other Letters, Vowels or Consonants, **only one accent** can get attached at a time.

Symbols having Indic Shaping class = **Special Function**
Geometric Shapes Block
- Dotted circle ◌ U+25CC = to show a missing base glyph
- No-break Space U+00A0 = to prevent dotted cirle
- Zero Width Non-Joiner U+200C = to prevent conjunct glyph
- Zero Width Joiner U+200D = to prevent half-forms glyph

Vedic Tone Marks having Indic Shaping class = **Cantillation**
Vedic Extensions Block **Dependent NonSpacing Mark**
- U+1CD0 – 1CD2 = attach above cantillation marks
- U+1CD5 – 1CD9 = attach below cantillation marks
- U+1CDA – 1CDB = attach above cantillation marks
- U+1CDC – 1CDF = attach below cantillation marks
- U+1CE0 = attach above cantillation mark
- U+1CF4 = attach above cantillation mark
- U+1CF8 – 1CF9 = attach above cantillation marks

Vedic Punctuations having Indic Shaping class = **None**
Vedic Extensions Block **Independent Punctuation**
- U+1CD3 = independent symbol

Vedic Mark having Indic Shaping class = **Cantillation**
Vedic Extensions Block **Dependent Mark**
- U+1CD4 = special svarita

Vedic Mark having Indic Shaping class = **Cantillation**
Vedic Extensions Block **Independent Spacing Mark**
- U+1CE1 = independent svarita

Vedic Marks having Indic Shaping class = **Avagraha**
Vedic Extensions Block Dependent Mark
- U+1CE2 – 1CE8 = attach to visarga

Vedic Other Letters having Indic Shaping class = **Symbol**
Vedic Extensions Block **Independent Other Letter**
- U+1CE9 – 1CEC = independent gomukha anusvara symbols, should be like base glyphs for Bindu to get attached.

Vedic Marks having Indic Shaping class = **Avagraha**
Vedic Extensions Block **Dependent Mark**
- U+1CED = tiryak that attachs below gomukha anusvaras

Vedic Other Letters having Indic Shaping class = **Symbol**
Vedic Extensions Block **Independent Other Letter**
- U+1CEE – 1CF1 = independent long anusvara symbols

Vedic Letters having Indic Shaping class = **Consonant_Dead**
Vedic Extensions Block **Independent Other Letter**
- U+1CF2 – 1CF3 = ardhavisarga, *should be dependent marks*

Vedic Mark having Indic Shaping class = **None**
Vedic Extensions Block **Independent Spacing Mark**
- U+1CF7 = atikrama symbol

Vedic Other Letter having Indic Shaping class = **Symbol**
Vedic Extensions Block **Independent Other Letter**
- U+1CFA = independent double gomukha anusvara symbol

Vedic Marks having Indic Shaping class = **Cantillation**
Devanagari Extended Block **Dependent NonSpacing Mark**
- U+A8E0 – A8E9 = combining numerals, position top
- U+A8EA – A8F0 = combining letters, position top
- U+A8F1 = combining avagraha, position top

Vedic Letters having Indic Shaping class = **Symbol**
Devanagari Extended Block **Independent Other Letter**
- U+A8F2 – A8F7 = long candrabindu symbols

Vedic Punctuations having Indic Shaping class = **None**
Devanagari Extended Block **Other Punctuation Mark**
- U+A8F8 – A8FA = vedic punctuations, independent symbols
- U+A8FC = vedic sacred symbol, independent symbol

Vedic Symbol having Indic Shaping class = **None**
Devanagari Extended Block **Other Letter Symbols**
- U+A8FB = vedic symbol, independent symbol

Vedic Symbol having Indic Shaping class = **None**
Devanagari Extended Block **Other Letter Symbols**
- U+A8FD = jain sacred symbol, independent symbol

Vedic Letter having Indic Shaping class = **Vowel**
Devanagari Extended Block **Independent Other Letter**
- U+A8FE = vowel symbol, independent symbol

Vedic Mark having Indic Shaping class = **Vowel Matra**
Devanagari Extended Block **Dependent NonSpacing Mark**
- U+A8FF = combining vowel matra

References

https://www.ashtangayoga.info/philosophy/sanskrit-and-devanagari/transliteration-tool/
https://www.learnsanskrit.cc/
https://scriptsource.org/
https://scriptsource.org/cms/scripts/page.php?item_id=wrSys_detail&key=sa-Deva
https://scriptsource.org/cms/scripts/page.php?item_id=language_detail_font&key=san
https://scriptsource.org/cms/scripts/page.php?item_id=script_detail&key=Deva

Latin Transliteration
https://en.wikipedia.org/wiki/International_Alphabet_of_Sanskrit_Transliteration
https://scriptsource.org/cms/scripts/page.php?item_id=entry_detail&uid=g8w4snzcy5
https://cdn.standards.iteh.ai/samples/28333/a0a778b7b2034a91aab1e97b3a34d125/ISO-15919-2001.pdf
https://www.lexilogos.com/keyboard/sanskrit_conversion.htm

Unicode Standard Version 4.0 dated Aug 2003
https://www.unicode.org/versions/Unicode4.0.0/ch09.pdf

Unicode Standard Version 13.0 dated Mar 2020
Chapter 12 South and Central Asia-I Official Scripts of India
https://www.unicode.org/versions/Unicode13.0.0/ch12.pdf

Unicode Standard Version 14.0 dated Sept 2021
https://www.unicode.org/versions/Unicode14.0.0/ch12.pdf

Unicode Standard Version 15.0 dated Sept 2022
https://www.unicode.org/versions/Unicode15.0.0/ch12.pdf

Sanskrit Devanagari Font List
https://list.indology.info/pipermail/indology/attachments/20230805/cdea9f08/attachment.htm

Font Sanskrit 2020
https://sourceforge.net/projects/advaita-sharada-font/files/Devanagari/

Font Sanskrit 2003 https://www.oah.in/Sanskrit/itranslator2003.htm
https://www.oah.in/Sanskrit/Sanskrit2003_30.07.2019.zip
Font Annapurna SIL https://software.sil.org/annapurna/
Font Arial Unicode MS https://www.download-free-fonts.com/details/88978/arial-unicode-ms
Font Lohit Devanagari
https://github.com/google/fonts/blob/master/ofl/lohitdevanagari/Lohit-Devanagari.ttf
Font CDAC Dhruv, Yogesh, Sakal Bharati
https://www.cdac.in/index.aspx?id=dl_sakal_bharati_font
Font Siddhanta http://svayambhava.blogspot.com/p/siddhanta-devanagariunicode-open-type.html
Font Chandas Uttara http://www.sanskritweb.net/cakram/
Google Noto https://fonts.google.com/noto/fonts?noto.query=dev
Font Adishila https://adishila.com/fonts/
Font Shobhika https://www.kramasubramanian.com/resources/shobhika
Font Gentium https://software.sil.org/gentium/charset/
Fonts Sanskrit https://www.omniglot.com/bloggle/?p=621
Fonts List http://www.devanaagarii.net/fonts/

Text Shaping Engine Microsoft Uniscribe
https://learn.microsoft.com/en-us/typography/develop/processing-part1
https://learn.microsoft.com/en-us/typography/script-development/devanagari
https://learn.microsoft.com/en-us/typography/tools/volt/
https://www.unicode.org/L2/L2021/21112-deva-cluster-valid.pdf
https://lindenbergsoftware.com/en/notes/issues-in-devanagari-cluster-validation/
https://simoncozens.github.io/fonts-and-layout/features-2.html#mark-positioning
https://learn.microsoft.com/en-us/typography/script-development/devanagari#shaping-engine

https://www.icann.org/sites/default/files/lgr/lgr-4-devanagari-script-05nov20-en.html

Devanagari Scripts (deva) and (dev2) Shaping Engine
https://github.com/n8willis/opentype-shaping-documents/blob/master/opentype-shaping-devanagari.md#distinctions-from-dev2

Text Shaping Engine Microsoft Directwrite
https://learn.microsoft.com/en-us/windows/win32/directwrite/direct-write-portal

Text Shaping Engine Apple Coretext
https://developer.apple.com/documentation/coretext/

Text Shaping Engine Adobe InDesign
https://helpx.adobe.com/in/indesign/kb/shaping-engine-world-ready-composer.html
https://helpx.adobe.com/in/photoshop/using/unified-text-engine.html

Text Shaping Engine Android Chrome Harfbuzz
https://github.com/harfbuzz/harfbuzz

Designing Devanagari Typefaces
https://designwithfontforge.com/en-US/Designing_Devanagari_Typefaces.html

Font Editors
https://fontforge.org/en-US/
https://www.high-logic.com/font-editor/fontcreator
https://glyphsapp.com/
https://www.glyphrstudio.com/
https://www.fontlab.com/

Font Forum
https://typedrawers.com/discussion/3870/attaching-a-devanagari-vedic-extensions-base-glyph-with-a-mark

https://typography.guru/forums/topic/105460-adobe-devanagari-font/
https://typedrawers.com/discussion/4360/indic-shaping-issue-in-devanagari-font

Text Editors
https://www.libreoffice.org/
https://www.microsoft.com/en/microsoft-365/
https://www.latex-project.org/

https://www.lexilogos.com/keyboard/sanskrit_vedic.htm
https://www.w3.org/International/ilreq/devanagari/

Keyboard Editors
https://www.kbdedit.com/
https://www.kbdedit.com/manual/ex23_sanskrit_with_vedic_extensions.html
https://help.keyman.com/
https://help.keyman.com/keyboard/sil_devanagari_phonetic/1.4/sil_devanagari_phonetic
https://ubcsanskrit.ca/keyboards.html
https://kbdlayout.info/KBDINDEV/
https://kevincarmody.com/software/aksharapad.html
https://mywhatever.com/home/sanskrit/vidyut/
https://www.alanwood.net/unicode/vedic-extensions.html

Ashwini Kumar Aggarwal
– Sanskrit Sandhi Handbook – 1st – 2019 –
– The Sanskrit Alphabet with Vedic Extensions – 1st – 2021 –
Devotees of Sri Sri Ravi Shankar Ashram, Punjab.

Epilogue

Sing freely.
Sing from your Soul.
Sing whenever you want.

Offer all to Her and rest deeply.

सर्वे भवन्तु सुखिनः । सर्वे सन्तु निरामयाः ।
सर्वे भद्राणि पश्यन्तु । मा कश्चिद् दुःख भाग् भवेत् ॥
ॐ शान्तिः शान्तिः शान्तिः ॥

When faith has blossomed in life, Every step is led by the Divine.
Sri Sri Ravi Shankar

Om Namah Shivaya

जय गुरुदेव

www.ingramcontent.com/pod-product-compliance
Lightning Source LLC
LaVergne TN
LVHW021337080526
838202LV00004B/209